soothe

how to find calm amid everyday chaos

jim brickman

RODALE.

Rodale books may be purchased for business or promotional use or for special sales. For information, please write to:

Special Markets Department, Rodale Inc., 733 Third Avenue, New York, NY 10017

Printed in the United States of America

Rodale Inc. makes every effort to use acid-free ∞, recycled paper ♻.

Book design by Joanna Williams

Library of Congress Cataloging-in-Publication Data is on file with the publisher.

ISBN-13: 978-1-62336-500-4 hardcover

Distributed to the trade by Macmillan

2 4 6 8 10 9 7 5 3 1 hardcover

We inspire and enable people to improve their lives and the world around them.
rodalebooks.com

To my mom,

sally brickman,

for always being there,

for always believing and helping me

dream big

contents

introduction

"**M**r. Brickman, we have a problem," said the medical technician.

Those are not the words anyone wanted to hear heading into an MRI exam for a knee that was causing pain. At age 50, I had searing pain, a date with a claustrophobia-inducing machine, and a nervous-looking health care pro in my midst.

Wait just a second. Why was she feeling anxious? It was *my* knee.

Naturally, my internal stress indicator was registering high alert. What problem? Was there a big issue? Was my fall worse than I thought? Was my knee beyond repair? Would I walk with a limp? Would I walk out of here? I might appear calm and collected on stage, but the truth is, I freak out. My first reaction is to assume the worst.

I guess maybe I'm a stress junkie because I live on it. Feed off it. And I've behaved like this for most of my adult life.

In this case, all of my worrying was needless.

"As you know, Mr. Brickman, we're about to take you in for your MRI, and some people get sort of wigged-out," said the friendly technician. "You know, claustrophobia. Do you suffer from it?" I didn't tell her I live on a tour bus for a big chunk of the year. I'm used to tin cans.

"Anyway," the technician continued. "I've found that one thing really helps my patients relax. In fact, it works every time. It's the music we play for almost everyone who has an MRI here, and it works wonders, but I'm not sure you want me to play it for you."

"Why wouldn't I want music that relaxes me?" I inquired. I love all kinds of music, and I was pretty sure they weren't going to be playing heavy metal.

"This is really funny. In fact, you'll get a good laugh from this—I hope. The thing is, it's *your* music," she said. "In fact, we absolutely love your music around here. People find it quite soothing."

Maybe for others. The truth is, I don't really listen to my own music in my free time.

Maybe today is a good time to start, I thought to myself, taking a deep breath, and not just because they were about to jam my body into a scary machine. I knew in that moment that as someone known for soothing others, I needed to take a closer look at the concept and make it a priority in my own crazy-busy life.

Of course, I had a good laugh when the medical technician insisted she would play "me" to me while they got some pictures of my banged-up leg.

Just like anyone else, I felt my own stress levels rise when they put me into that big metal machine for almost an hour. Of course, I knew it was mind over matter in there, but I wasn't really sure if I was ready to surrender to the moment and find a happier place in my mind.

For those of you who haven't had an MRI, the machine is really loud. So there I was, lying flat on my back and feeling totally claustrophobic.

Then the tech put on one of my tracks. I heard the bright sound of the tinkling piano keys, and my first thought was *Gee, maybe I should play this song in concert more often. It's a good one.* A few minutes went by and I evaluated another song. *That's a beautiful song,* I thought and then immediately felt guilty. Is it acceptable to say your own song is beautiful?

Finally I just had to let go.

It was like being on a plane sitting next to the kid who's screaming the loudest. At first you're anxious, but then you just have to go into your own zone where the kid and his noise melt away. It didn't take long before I was in my zone, soothing out to the rest of the tracks.

In a strange way, I didn't want that feeling to end, although I could have done without the MRI part.

It was a real wake-up call.

And so it began. Over the next two years, I embarked on a journey to find the tools to calm down, a journey that has now become the basis for this book. So take a deep breath and learn how to soothe yourself in ways you never expected.

Hi, my name is Jim Brickman, and for those of you who don't know about me, I'm a stressaholic. I have to smile while writing that because to earn a living I play the piano in concert halls around the globe, and beautiful music and stress are not supposed to go together. Playing the piano, whether at home by myself or on stage in front of a crowd, has always been the easy part for me. It's in my DNA. The truth is, playing music and the business of the music industry are two completely different animals. Ask any performer; we all have our own stress routines.

It wasn't always that way.

My fingers hit the keyboard for the first time when I was 4. Three years later I began taking private lessons from Mrs. T, a piano teacher down the street from my family's Shaker Heights, Ohio, home. In those days, it didn't take long for me to completely stress out that nice lady who was teaching music. For some reason, I just wouldn't conform to the rudiments of piano playing, which in her eyes was playing the music exactly the way it was written on the page.

Oh, how I tormented Mrs. T from down the street. I couldn't seem to help myself. Even at a young age, I knew the music and the techniques she was teaching me had no nuance to them. Eventually Mrs. T—my sweet, well-meaning piano teacher—ended up telling my mother, "I'm so sorry, Mrs. Brickman, but your son just doesn't have the knack for piano playing. His rhythm is all over the place. He doesn't focus. I don't see the point in continuing these lessons."

Well, my mother didn't give up easily. She was the one who saw me playing on the only piano we had in our house, which was made out of felt. In fact, it was a felt strip with all the keys drawn on it; obviously no real music was coming out of those fibers—and the tunes were the result of my active imagination. It was my most prized possession and I taught myself the basics on it. Mom knew this wasn't the time to walk away from the piano, even though we were a long way off from a baby grand in the living room.

Thanks, Mom. Without you, none of this would have been possible. It all adds up to a career that makes me proud when I stop to think about it—which I don't do often. Most of the time I'm like anyone else out there who beats herself or himself up for not achieving more in the 24 hours we call a day. Add a little airplane travel to the mix along with interviews, plus dealing with aging parents and family, and you have the modern-day stress cocktail. Just add ice. Wait, do I even have ice? Did I remember to call the fridge repairman? Right, that's on tomorrow's list.

Do you ever have that feeling where you're mentally, not to mention physically, extremely stressed out by the end of each day? Do you ever think that you're not moving ahead but just maintaining? Are you treading water in your own stress pool, barely keeping your head above the surface?

Those questions and many more like them bring me to this book. In *Soothe*, I'm going to share with you the story of how a stressed-out pop artist learned to jump off the stress hamster wheel. The funny thing is, I may seem like an unlikely spokesperson for a book on soothing, but for those who have heard my radio show or seen my live performances, it makes perfect sense. The truths contained in this book are hard-won. Let me emphasize that in the last two years, I've made a conscious decision to find real ways to limit my stress and find soothing moments. To that end, I've found creative, easy, inexpensive, and unique ways to calm down amid the chaos—and you can do the same. On these pages, I describe what works and what doesn't when it comes to soothing your life.

I also asked for a little help from my friends. Each week I interview experts from all walks of life on my syndicated radio show, *Your Weekend with Jim Brickman*, and they're so friendly and helpful that when I called them up and asked for a few tips for this book, they were more than happy to contribute. Their personal soothing techniques have been life changers for me and my audience on the radio. I'm thrilled to bring even more tips and solutions to the page—look for their tips in the "Soothe Expert" sidebars strewn throughout the book.

Each chapter features one of my major life lessons along with concrete ways to alleviate stress and soothe yourself back to a place of tranquility or as close to that nirvana as possible in our chaotic world. I don't imagine you retreating to sit in a cross-legged position in a quiet room on a mountaintop and chanting *Om*, but instead see you soothing yourself when you feel the pressure start to build during your everyday activities. Maybe for you that's the minute you walk into the house and five people pull you in different directions, or it's in the supermarket line when that lady cuts you off. Perhaps you'll use one of my tips to deal with an overly demanding boss or an elderly parent or a partner who just picked a little fight.

The lessons I share will pinpoint stresses that involve work, health, family, love, aging parents, getting older, diet, exercise, expectations, personal judgments, unforeseen circumstances, and that universal question: "Is this all there is?"

This book is packed with practical ways to de-stress, including turning off your electronics and getting the right amount of restful sleep at night to repair your body and reboot for the next day. The solution to a good night's sleep might be simply lowering the temperature in your room just a couple of degrees.

Are you eating to reduce your natural body stressors? Are you allowing drama to seep into every area of your life? What can you do right now to soothe and unwind?

the soothing starts

Of course we can't change the world in one book, and there will still be those daily stressors that hit us hard. What I hope this book does for you is teach you how to recognize stress while it's happening, dial it down, and then evaluate exactly how much weight should be given to the situation in the first place.

Ask yourself: Are you so accustomed to living in stress that you don't know any other way at this point?

The simple truth is, you're the only one who can deal with your own stress. You give it power, and you can take that power away when it comes to your stress triggers.

It takes a conscious effort to manage our fast-paced

soothe now

Lesson One: Breathe in through your nose for a count of four and hold that for four, then breathe out through your mouth for a count of eight. Try that five times with your eyes closed.
    Feels great, doesn't it?

lifestyles these days. Not all of us have time for vacations or daily yoga. As you work through the tips in this book, I'll urge you to ask yourself: Do I really want to continue my stress-perpetuating habits, or would I rather make time to do something soothing, like going to a movie or taking a walk or cranking up the Rolling Stones?

I will also help you finally resolve the following questions:

Am I a bad person if I say no once in a while?

Should I internalize every twist and turn that happens?

Is my personal judgment meter making my blood pressure soar?

How do I ask for help—and is asking for help a bad thing?

Do I do anything at all to relax anymore? Or is it just wake up, work, handle the kids, watch TV, and then head off to bed—only to get up the next day and do it all over again?

This book is about taking your life back.

1

soothe your stress

Are you stressed? In our busy world, it's almost a badge of honor to walk around saying, "I'm so stressed out!" Can you imagine calling a friend and saying, "Everything is great. I'm calm pretty much all of the time. Life is a breeze"? Your friend would probably say, "Who exactly *is* this on the phone?"

In our busy, overscheduled lives, it's almost a given that we're walking around frazzled. On my holiday tour, I might hit 30 cities in 30 days, but that's what I love to do. Nothing makes me happier during the warmth of the holiday season than sitting down at the piano in front of all my fans and playing my songs along with some Christmas classics. Am I stressed that I have to leave the theater, hop on a plane, avoid a snowstorm, deal with missing luggage, and then figure out where the heck the hotel is in the middle of a dark night in

Portland? Of course I might be juggling a lot, but the truth is, I'm a pretty happy guy doing what I believe I was born to do. So, to answer my own question: I'm crazy busy with my life, which can be stressful at times.

I was talking with a woman at one of my concerts the other day and she told me that she took a buyout from her company during the recession. She remarked how suddenly stress-free her life was these days. "What are you up to now?" I asked her.

"Well, I'm gardening and going to my club five days a week. I've been doing yoga. That's pretty much it," she said, sounding a little guilty as she rattled off her daily list. Her regular life in the past included traveling, working weekends, and regularly dealing with Chicago O'Hare shutdowns because of snowstorms. I wanted to know: Was she feeling guilty for being forced to remove the stress from her life? "Jim, I do feel kind of bad about it. I tell my friends who are juggling kids and jobs how I actually have free time. It's like they don't want to hear about it. One of my friends even said, 'How *nice* for you. I gotta go.'"

how do you know if you're stressed?

The other day I decided to try a little experiment to see how stressed I was. I've read so much about how nature is naturally de-stressing, so I went for a walk with a friend—a friend who is much more Zen than I am. It was one of those beautiful

soothe now

Ask yourself: Are you so focused on your "stuff" that you don't see what's happening to you?

spring days when the air is cool but there's just a hint of a warm breeze. We grabbed some lunch and took a walk past trees in bloom all around us. "Hey, look at that cute little puppy," said my friend. "Huh?" I remarked because I hadn't even noticed the dog. "The petunias are blooming. They really look nice," said my friend. Petunias? What petunias? Oh, right, those petunias over there ... and over there ... *and over there*. I hadn't really noticed them.

There is a good chance you're stressed if you walk around caught up in your own head and don't really see much around you. I have a way of being in my head even when I'm seemingly enjoying what's around me. I'm a pro at coasting absent-mindedly through every moment or mindlessly remarking about something without really looking at it and certainly not finding joy in it. I can converse with someone else while thinking about other things. I can't help it. My mind races as I try to problem-solve and multitask even while on a supposedly de-stressing walk.

Try spending time with a Zen friend and practice pushing away whatever else is in your mind. Let yourself look for the details: those purple flowers, the lady with the weird floppy hat, that young couple having a picnic and making out in the grass. Instead of thinking, *Oh, cute young love. But I really have to get to the bank and I wonder why Mom is calling—I hope she's okay,* force yourself to think just about the couple. How old are they? What is their story? What is she wearing? Is this a new relationship? An old one? Do I have that? Do I want that?

Experts agree that when you get out of your own head and focus on someone else or something else, your entire system takes everything down one notch and you truly begin to relax. In fact, helping others is a great way to get out of your own headspace of negativity and stress. Of course, I'm not saying that you should do good things just to reap the benefits yourself!

This reminds me of a remarkable young man named Zach Sobiech, 17, who was diagnosed with a rare form of bone cancer and was told he had only months to live. Instead of dwelling on his own situation and focusing on the obvious stress, Zach did something that took an incredible amount of courage. He thought of the others in his life, the people he loved, and put those feelings into a song called "Clouds," which is about hope and promise. Through his story, he knew he could inspire others going through hard times, and he could have a meaningful impact on this world.

After he died, I did a concert in Minnesota that benefited the Zach Sobiech Osteosarcoma Fund. That night, Zach's family attended and came up on stage to perform Zach's song "Clouds." This touching experience compelled me to record a version of "Clouds" for my last album. I wanted to honor Zach's legacy, wanted to help him send out into the world this song that taught us that even in the darkest moments, there are ways to take the focus off what's bad and find what's good and positive. I love the lyrics of his song: "And we'll go up, up, up / But I'll fly a little higher / We'll go up in the clouds because the view is a little nicer / Up here my dear."

How trivial my stress seemed when I was immersed in getting this important young man's message out. I can't thank Zach enough for putting things into perspective and reminding me of what's truly important. I know that during the days in which I was recording "Clouds," I didn't allow life's minor annoyances to shake me.

What might you accomplish when you get out of your own drama, or when you see how you can be of service to others by honoring them, helping them, or passing on their important message?

To read more about Zach Sobiech's story and to hear "Clouds," visit SootheYourWorld.com.

signs of stress

Here's a quick cheat sheet when it comes to deciding exactly how stressed you are. Remember that stress can cause mental and physical health issues, including high blood pressure and heart-related issues. Here are a few physical symptoms of stress and anxiety that you should pay attention to in your quest to figure out how stressed you are:

You might be stressed if:

○ **You have frequent headaches.** When you're stressed, you clench your jaw or tense your facial muscles. You also tense your neck and shoulders, which leads to headaches. You might also grind your teeth. Check with your doctor if symptoms persist.

○ **It hurts all over.** Maybe you don't have a headache, but after a stressful day, you feel like you just had a major workout at a gym. Your muscles ache and you might think that you're coming down with something. The next day you're fine. This could be stress, which works on your nervous system. When you're stressed, your natural flight-or-fight response kicks in and then blood rushes to major muscle groups. This muscle tension causes you to clench up and your muscles to tighten. This makes them feel sore and painful later on or stay tight, which is painful.

○ **Your stomach aches.** You were feeling fine, and suddenly your stomach starts churning and you feel a killer stomachache developing. Kids will often seem fine in the evening but in the morning say they have a tummy ache and don't want to go to school. A lot of the time, the pain your kid is feeling is real and he or she is not just making stuff up to stay home and play video games—he or she might be stressed! Many people find that their stress transitions into stomach cramps, diarrhea, constipation, nausea, and a generally upset stomach.

○ **Your face breaks out.** Why do teens break out so frequently? Some believe it's their stress levels. This also explains why middle-age people can also suddenly have a few zits. Stress ups your level of the hormone cortisol, which then produces more testosterone. This has been known to cause acne.

○ **You have reddish skin and eczema.** When you're stressed, your skin can reveal it. Why? Stress leads to inflammation, which can cause a reddish complexion and even eczema.

○ **You feel sweaty.** Stress causes us to sweat, which might just stress you out more. Sweat is a result of your flight-or-fight response, which triggers hormones such as adrenaline.

○ **You can't sleep.** It's well known that stress not only gives you restless sleep, which leaves you exhausted and more stressed out, but also increases rapid eye movement (REM) sleep and thus decreases your slow-wave or deep sleep. The result? Your body doesn't get to do cell repair, which leaves you weaker, vulnerable to diseases, and exhausted.

○ **You invite disease.** When you're really stressed, your hormones run amok and your immune system is compromised. What happens next is that your body has trouble producing the white blood cells that fight off diseases and infection. This leaves you susceptible to all sorts of illnesses.

(continued on page 12)

soothe expert:

Dr. Drew Ramsey on Stress

I can't say enough about Dr. Drew Ramsey, who is an assistant clinical professor of psychiatry at Columbia University and a frequent guest on my radio show, *Your Weekend with Jim Brickman*. He studies how the brain functions and has written several books about it, which makes him a perfect *Soothe* expert. He also has a clinical practice in which he helps patients find greater happiness by focusing on what is causing their brain to stay happy and eliminating what's making them not so thrilled about life. Here are his tips for dealing with daily stress.

MANAGE YOUR STRESS

Stress is unavoidable. The main focus for all of us should be how to manage stress in better, more effective ways. We can intervene in a biological way to make sure we have a brain that is reacting to our stressors optimally. A good example is to imagine yourself running out of the house in the morning, having had no breakfast. You're too busy for lunch. It's two o'clock in the afternoon now and you haven't eaten a thing. The kids are crying. You're driving in traffic. And you're more reactive than ever and more irritable or on edge. Talk about a bad mood. Are you stressed? The truth is, you're probably hungry, which is making you irritable. So in this case, we can say you're stressed because you're hungry. Remember that biology drives your stress because your brain is either managing stress or not.

DEAL WITH STRESSORS

You really need to develop your own personal psychological toolbox, which is why the tips in this book are great. All of us have to pay our bills. We have to say difficult things to another person. Most of us deal with bosses. Things break in the house. People die. The road of life is paved with bumps. That is a given. But there are ways to raise your awareness and mindfulness and learn how to soothe yourself.

SOOTHE YOURSELF

I am in New York City and see some of the most overscheduled people on the planet. Sometimes people will focus on everything but themselves, and they also avoid the truth. I saw a man recently who told me he was a good father figure. I asked him how much time a month he spent with his son, and he told me on average about one day a month—hardly a model parent. People like to avoid really sitting with themselves and their feelings. Our modern lives and addiction to electronics help us be avoidant. You can't avoid soothing just because life is stressful.

The first thing I do when I find myself in a stressed state is to think about what nourishment I've taken in that day. I collect the data. Let's say I went to a party the night before and feel bad the next morning. I know I need breakfast and hydration. The next time you're stressed, ask yourself: "Am I hungry? Angry? Lonely?" Then remedy that problem, and as you directly address the source, you might just find your stress melting away.

QUELL HUNGER TO FIGHT STRESS

I hate the idea of "stress eating," as you need the right fuel to combat stress and take on life's challenges. Eating can be a wonderful tool to combat stress. During times of stress, I make sure to give myself a healthy snack like a kale salad, a piece of dark chocolate, or a handful of almonds. Nourishing foods help shift your mental state. I also like spicy foods when stressed. A black bean taco with extra hot sauce is soothing in the afternoon when your energy is low and you need nutrients and energy.

DON'T PANIC

My number one tip for immediate de-stressing and soothing? Stop the catastrophic thinking. It's not the end of the world. The thing I see the most in my office is catastrophic thinking. Your house won't be foreclosed on because a payment is late. It's usually not bad news from the doctor when the phone rings. Just because the school called doesn't mean there was an accident—maybe your child won an award. Keep it all in context and remember that it's usually not the worst-case scenario.

soothe now
WITH MINDFUL BREATHING

When I asked for his favorite way to soothe patients who are particularly stressed out, Dr. Drew cited mindful breathing as a tool that's particularly useful. Some people call this a cleansing breath. It doesn't matter what you call this technique. It works, and it can be done anywhere at almost any time.

- Inhale through your nose (through one nostril if you can by blocking one nostril with your finger). Inhale to a count of four beats.
- As you inhale through your nose, feel your abdomen, lungs, and chest fill with air.

- Focus on your breath alone. If random thoughts (Bills! Kids! Layoffs!) happen to drift into your head, treat them like unwanted interruptions and let them pass.
- Purse your lips and exhale through your mouth to a count of eight beats.
- Repeat on the other nostril (or again if you didn't block your nostril).

Dr. Drew explains that you always want to exhale longer than you inhale. If you inhale slowly and then push all the air out, you're blowing too harshly and you won't soothe your system. By pursing your lips, you actually slow down your breath. "This type of breath instantly changes your physiology," says Dr. Drew. "This is a perfect exercise to do when you're feeling anxious. Anxiety heightens our stress response and our heart rate goes up. Our breathing becomes rapid. You want to slow down the breath to calm down."

He recalls a certain patient who came to his office to talk about love issues. "He was telling me about a fight he'd had with his girlfriend. I counted to 45 before the man even took a breath. So basically, this man was stressed out . . . and then was stressing himself out even more by not breathing," Dr. Drew explains. "With the breath inhalation, focus on pulling in good positive energy, nourishment, and white light, which is a calming force. The breath also fuels your brain with oxygen. You're pulling in this life force." Because of this, if you don't breathe regularly and mindfully, you'll be even more stressed.

○ **Things are not so hot in the bedroom.** Why is it that when we're stressed out, the last thing on earth we want to think about is sex—a major stress reducer? Medically speaking, this is absolutely normal because stress lowers your gonadotropin-releasing hormone (GnRH), which incidentally is the body's main sex hormone. You're looking at reduced sperm count, ovulation, and sexual activity, too. This is why couples who are trying to conceive a baby are always told not to stress out about it.

○ **You have panic attacks.** In some people, stress causes symptoms that can make it feel like a heart attack is coming on. It's always good to seek immediate medical attention if this is your situation, as you want to make sure it isn't your heart. Doctors might tell you that you're having a panic attack; in medical terms, your baseline arousal level is running on high.

Remember that chronic stress needs attention. If you live in a state of stress, you might have an anxiety disorder, which requires professional care. Check with your doc, who might recommend working with a psychologist, counselor, or psychiatrist.

build your soothing toolbox

To start soothing, try to put the following into practice today:

- Stay hydrated and drink water, not just caffeinated beverages.
- Regulate your blood sugar by eating whole foods and make sure you're never hungry by incorporating healthy snacks into your diet.
- Avoid white sugars, which cause your blood sugar to spike and then fall.
- Move. Any exercise, including walking, immediately soothes you.
- Focus on relaxing breathing techniques.

2

soothe your mornings

First, a confession: Ever since I hit 40, I've had a really hard time waking up in the morning. I used to pop right out of bed ready to greet the day. So what happened? Maybe it's age or more responsibility. I'm not popping up anymore.

In fact I'm just like anyone else who is completely exhausted and really loves a good sleep. That's why the blinging and buzzing of my smartphone alarm is my enemy. A hotel wake-up call on tour is even worse.

Before I became focused on soothing, I'd wake up in a funk, breathe, check the clock, and then think about my day. I'd sit with my feet dangling from the end of the bed planning out the next 12 stressful hours in my mind while trying to figure out if and when I could fit in the gym and a few meals.

In other words, I'd be awake less than a minute and out of habit I'd begin the Jim Brickman stress routine.

Most of us know that exact stress drill. The minute the alarm bleeps, beats, or blips, you're well into your day—at least mentally.

I wondered: How can you soothe yourself before your day even starts?

do not plug in, look up, or check it out

I'm not a late sleeper. Most days I'm up at 7 a.m. Maybe I'll go to 8 a.m. at the latest. I don't think I've ever slept to 10 on a weekday, because I just couldn't. Why? I have such anxiety about missing something because I'm conditioned to actually hear Claire, my manager, in my office saying, "Jim, how in the world could you sleep in? You have a phone interview!" Of course, missing fictional phone interviews and worrying about this stuff is a problem, which is why I asked some experts about how to start my day off in a better way.

Thus began my new way of facing the morning.

There is nothing that says "modern morning" like waking up to check your e-mails and phone messages. May I suggest that you wake up and NOT CHECK ANYTHING until after you drink your first glass of water? This doesn't mean you keep a large glass of water by the bed to subvert this plan. Make an honest attempt to leave the electronics in the kitchen, or if you need to keep them around you in case of emergency, then just don't check them until you're really awake.

Compare these two possible scenarios:

Stressed: Your alarm screams and you start awake. Your eyelids are still heavy. Your mind can't believe it's already 6:00 a.m. You just checked the time a few minutes ago when the dog rolled over and it was still dark. Wait, it *is* still dark. You roll over, but not to embrace a significant other or even to check the weather outside your bedroom window. Instead, you let your fingers caress your iPhone. Before your feet hit the floor, you're checking messages. *Oh no! Your mom called. Is it a problem? Oh no! Why didn't that overnight package arrive? Oh no! I have two meetings at the same time today! Oh no! What does my bank want now?* Before your feet hit the floor, you are already on stress overload.

Soothed: Your alarm rings, and it's a lovely Brickman tune (sorry, had to do it). You love the song and don't want to turn it off (sorry again). You roll over and your fingers caress your dog, cat, partner, or fluffy comforter. You make your way out of bed without checking anything and do a few quick stretches, hit the bathroom, and take a relaxing shower. You've been up for 20 minutes now and everything is pretty good. You're waking up slowly, and you glance outside to see that it's sunny. That makes you happy.

I know you're saying, "Jim, come on! I have to check my messages." Let me suggest that you make it all the way to the kitchen. Pour a glass of water, and then if you must, check your phone or e-mail. If you can handle it, why not turn on some great music, eat a little breakfast, and *then* check? The point is to put off checking as long as possible. It's seven in the morning. Whatever happened last night on your e-mail can wait a few more minutes.

(continued on page 20)

soothe expert:

Dr. Drew Ramsey on Fueling Your Brain and Body in the A.M.

Breakfast really is the most important meal of the day. But for most of us, mornings tend to be rushed, busy, and stressful, and eating healthfully is often the last thing on our minds. I checked in with Dr. Drew for some quick fixes to get every day started off right.

FEEL LIKE A HERO WITH SUPER FOODS

Eating foods packed with two key ingredients—protein and fiber—means you'll have more energy to deal with the day ahead. Here are a few simple ideas to supercharge your breakfast:

- Pumpkin seeds are filled with zinc and magnesium. Sprinkle them on your oatmeal to stay calm and focused all day.
- Skip the margarine and grab a jar of almond butter to spread on toast or a bagel for a great dose of healthy fats and vitamin E.
- My big fat Greek yogurt! Not only is yogurt easy to eat on-the-go, it's also filled with protein and bacteria (the good kind!) that helps improve digestion and boosts immunity.
- Go green with an avocado—add to your morning smoothie or mix in with eggs for a natural metabolism booster.

JUST SAY NO TO SUGAR

Even though that extra-large caramel frappuccino is tempting, too much sugar is dangerous—it's the ultimate "empty calorie" that's bad for your brain and packs on the pounds. Try green tea, which is naturally caffeinated and also boosts metabolism. Sweeten with honey or Stevia. Or, jumpstart your morning with an all-natural, satisfying smoothie. If it's bottled, make sure there's less than 25 grams of sugar per 8 ounces.

SNACK AWAY ON THE GOOD STUFF

If you need to satisfy cravings in-between meals, there's no better snack than a handful of nature's bounty. Berries are packed with antioxidants, and high in fiber, which makes you feel fuller longer. If you've had your fill of strawberries, blackberries, and blueberries, try goji berries—it's been said that they're a fountain of youth! Or, grab a bag of unsalted nuts for a perfectly portable snack. Nuts are also high in fiber, and part of a heart-healthy diet.

Cheesy Scrambled Eggs and Kale   Serves 4

If you have a little more time to prepare breakfast at home, treat yourself to this deliciously simple dish from Dr. Drew's book, *50 Shades of Kale*. There's no need to stress about cholesterol—studies show that up to seven eggs a week won't affect your blood cholesterol levels. Eggscellent news!

6 eggs
1 tablespoon olive oil
5 ounces kale, trimmed and thinly sliced (about 5 cups)

Olive oil cooking spray
1 cup grated mozzarella or Colby cheese

Place the eggs in a medium bowl and whisk well. Set aside.

Heat a large skillet over medium heat. Add the olive oil and kale and cook for 2 to 3 minutes, pressing down on the kale with a metal lid, turning until it's soft.

Transfer the kale to a plate. Warm the same skillet (that you cooked the kale in) over medium-high heat. Coat with a thin layer of cooking spray.

Add the eggs and cook for 2 to 3 minutes, stirring often, until soft curds form. Add the kale and the cheese and remove from heat. Cover and rest for 1 minute, until the cheese melts. Serve immediately.

In my great unplugged-morning experiment, I tried for a week to actually turn off the phone before I went to bed. I dared myself to not turn it back on until 9:00 a.m., which is the start of the normal business day. I felt strange not to wake up with my phone, but I knew that we'd be canoodling all day long. It was also an amazing feeling; for once I felt in control of technology instead of the other way around.

When you're in control, you feel soothed. In my case, I employ other people. I had to trust my staff to handle things until I turned the phone on.

So far, I haven't missed any career or life-changing moments by not facing the morning with a first-thing phone fling.

yes, you should exercise in the morning

You can feed yourself breakfast, but are you feeding your mind in the morning? That jolt of coffee doesn't count because that's just artificial stimulation. Exercise actually increases the birth and development of new nerve cells in your brain, and these nerve cells are also the components of your brain that slow down and even die because of stress. A recent study shows that people who don't exercise much exhibit greater stress-related atrophy of the hippocampal area of the brain compared with those who are more physically active. You want to keep the stressors down because the hippocampus affects long- and short-term memory along with a myriad of other important functions.

If your brain isn't a good enough reason to hit the tread-mill or the jogging path in the morning, consider that exercise not only naturally lowers your stress levels but also increases your self-confidence because it jump-starts the production of endorphins (your feel-good boosters). Exercise actually helps you settle into a state of well-being, which is a great way to start the day, if you ask me.

According to a study at the University of Maryland, Baltimore, when you move even at a moderate pace, you release neuropeptides, brain chemicals that counteract the stress response. So get out there and get moving to start your day.

My favorite morning workout exercises include:

- **Plank.** A basic plank is supporting your body weight on your elbows and using your legs to lift off the ground until you're parallel with the floor. Keeping your core tight, hold for as long as you can. On really good days, I hold for upwards of two minutes. To make things more difficult, try rais-ing one foot off the floor and balancing on just your arms and the other foot, then switching feet.
- **Superman stretch.** In this exercise, you lie on your stomach and lift your arms and legs a few inches off the ground, mimicking Superman fly-ing in the sky. This is a yoga and Pilates move that really gets the blood flowing.
- **Corner stretch.** Stand facing the corner of your room. Raise your elbows to shoulder height. Place

your forearms, elbows, and palms against either wall in the corner. Now just lean in and flex your chest and back muscles. Hold for 15 seconds while breathing deeply. (You can also do this through-out the day when you feel stressed.)

○ **Push-ups.** I like these more than sit-ups for some reason. Every single day I like to add one more because it feels like I'm accomplishing something. Of course, eventually you could be doing thou-sands of push-ups, so I suggest sets of 10.

○ **Wall sit.** Stand with your back against a wall and your feet about a foot and a half in front of you. Slide down the wall until your legs create a 90-degree angle, making sure your knees do not move past your ankles. Hold for as long as you can!

○ **Suitcases.** Sit on the floor with your knees bent and your feet on the ground. Lift your feet off the ground so you're balancing on your bottom, and take your arms out to the side. To do one rep, straighten your legs out in front of you and take your back down until it almost touches the floor, then sit back up, keeping your feet off the floor the entire time. You're mimicking a suitcase opening and closing—and working up quite an ab burn!

○ **Stairs.** I'll think of a reason to go down to my basement and walk up and down the stairs several times. I make sure to take a couple of trips and bring something down with me each time. It's de-stressing because I'm working out and organizing my house at the same time.

○ **Walking.** I'll take a walk around my Cleveland neighborhood or a stroll in the park, or I'll walk to my office.

○ **Stretch.** Sit with your legs crossed in front of you. With a hand on either knee, push your knees gently toward the floor.

For a video of this workout and others, visit SootheYourWorld.com.

food that naturally de-stresses you in the morning

There is no getting out of it: You must eat breakfast. And just a cup of coffee won't do. I always eat breakfast, whether it's toast made from Ezekiel Sprouted Grain bread, a healthy shake, or some oatmeal. "After sleeping all night, our metabolism and blood sugar are at their lowest; we need a healthy breakfast to reenergize us," says Rebecca Scritchfield, RD, a nutritionist based in Washington, DC.

Okay, here comes the depressing news: You might want to consider cutting back on your java, which we all know can make us feel a little jumpy. Jumpy is not a great way to start a soothing day! A nutritionist advised me to switch to black tea, and then I read about a study by the University College London that showed that drinking black tea four times a week for six weeks can actually lower your cortisol levels even when you are stressed. That's a win-win.

Another one of my favorite beverages is green tea. For me, this was an acquired taste, but now I think it's just delicious. And it comes with great news: It contains L-theanine, which actually tells your brain to pour out great relaxation alpha waves while getting rid of nasty tense beta waves.

What about the rest of breakfast? You do have to eat it, because starting your day out hungry is stressful. The good news is there are many foods you can incorporate into your morning routine that are actually great at bringing stress levels down before your day begins. Try a few of my favorite foods that experts tell me naturally work on your stress levels. Personally, I like a smoothie or a serving of oatmeal (recipes on page 26), but I'm trying hard to make sure I have some of the Soothe Foods listed below in my breakfast choices to give me a little extra shot of calm.

Here's what researchers say to eat to help you keep your cool:

- **Nuts.** Full of magnesium, they work to keep your cortisol levels in check. If I'm running to an early morning flight, I will grab a handful of mixed nuts to take with me on the plane.

○ **Broccoli.** Not only is broccoli a great cancer fighter, but it also has folic acid, which helps you reduce stress. Keep your leftover steamed broccoli from the night before and add it to your omelet.

○ **Complex carbs.** Yes, you can have that whole grain in the morning because a modest portion of complex carbs (whole and sprouted grains or veggies) raises your serotonin levels, which puts you in a better mood and can even help you relax into your day. Plus, if you eat carbs early in the day, you're more likely to burn them off later.

○ **An LEO.** This is an omelet with lox (smoked salmon), eggs, and onions. The omega-3 fatty acids in the salmon actually help your brain cells function better together, thus enabling you to deal with stress in a more effective way. Plus, it's pretty delicious.

○ **Milk.** Yes, your mother was right. Even as an adult, you need your calcium. Milk also contains tryptophan, which, after it's metabolized, is turned into serotonin, which boosts your feel-good mood.

○ **Hot chocolate/tea.** Experts say that drinking something warm equals comfort and triggers a soothing feeling. I'll add just a hint of almond or coconut milk.

jim's favorite morning smoothie

Each day I like to create a different blend of ingredients. This provides variety and something to look forward to every morning.

1–2	cups spinach
½	cup coconut milk
1	cup water
½	cup ice
1	apple, cored and coarsely chopped
1	handful blueberries
1	large scoop green protein powder of your choice (I use Vega One)
1	tablespoon chia seeds
1	tablespoon flaxseeds

Put all the ingredients into a blender. Blend well.

jim's favorite morning oatmeal

I can't deal with steel-cut oats because I mess them (and the kitchen) up every single time. Instead, I just get Trader Joe's oatmeal with flaxseeds in it, which comes in individual packets. I'll top it with pure maple syrup or a protein such as almond butter or Greek yogurt. If I'm in the mood for sweets, I'll add a little chopped banana or some berries, but I steer clear of oatmeal flavored with brown sugar or apples.

Visit SootheYourWorld.com for more delicious smoothie recipes.

soothe now

Visit SootheYourWorld.com for a few songs I've picked that are great to listen to while you get going on your soothing morning.

Observers on my tour bus when I'm stirring up my morning oatmeal say, "Jim's making his concoction again"—though many now follow suit.

If I have a big day ahead of me, I'll do both the shake and the oatmeal. Or I'll save the oatmeal to eat as a morning snack.

turn off the news

I love starting my day catching up on the events of the world. Quite often I'm in a hotel room on tour and the first thing I like to do is turn on CNN or the *Today* show. I was curious when I read that this was often a tough way to start your day. Why? The news gets our blood pressure rising. It's hard to start your day off hearing that the economy is collapsing, your house is worth much less now, and soon gas is going to cost $10 a gallon. My personal favorite is the report that a huge snowstorm is gripping the East Coast—the exact place I need to be tomorrow to appear before a sold-out audience.

I read that taking a "morning news break" is a great way to start the day. Yes, it's great to watch that inspirational

soothe now

If it's possible, hug someone on your way out the door. Hugging not only transfers energy but gives both people involved an emotional lift.

feature about the kid who just saved 100 puppies. But when it comes to hard-core news, I've been trying to hit the mute button and catch up later.

Why? "Sometimes you need to take a temporary vacation from world events to clear your head, reduce your worries, and put your life in perspective," says Dr. Richard Blonna, a professor in the Department of Public Health at New Jersey's William Paterson University who specializes in stress management. "Most of the important stories will still be around next week. You can even go back and read them or watch them."

think positively about your day

It really is mind over matter when it comes to setting up your daily routine to handle stress. If you can force yourself to think, *It's going to be a good, productive day,* then more likely it will be just like you called it over breakfast. Science shows that thinking positively can moderate your stress.

I loved reading a 2010 Yale study in which students were actually coached by their professor to feel good, and even positively excited, before taking their graduate school entrance exams. He told them to not focus on the stress of the situation, but instead to wipe away that away like chalk being erased from a blackboard. The students were told to focus on positivity before their. Later, the professor compared these students to those who were not coached. Positive thinking did result in higher scores both during a practice test and later during the real exam.

The point is, start your day thinking about the good, which ensures that you walk out the door in a better mood, one directed toward happiness instead of hopelessness.

just breathe

This isn't just the name of a Pearl Jam song. Breathing in the right way is crucial when it comes to getting stress out of your system. I've learned that when you know it's going to be a tough day, nothing works better than taking a deep breath. In fact, this is the quickest and most direct way to calm down.

soothe now

Practice mindful breathing so it becomes second nature. It took me a while to get this right, but now it's easy. Just breathe in while imagining that your stomach is a balloon. You're slowly filling your balloon up with air. When you breathe out, don't force the air out, but exhale in a calm way as if you're allowing the air to gently leak out.

This works because it's the exact opposite of stress breathing. When you're stressed, your body is conditioned to breathe in short spurts from your chest. This type of breathing actually tells your central nervous system to release your stress hormones. Mindful breathing lowers your heart rate and helps deal with depression and anxiety, says Dr. Melinda Ring, medical director of integrative medicine at Northwestern Memorial Hospital in Chicago.

3

soothe your kingdom

A friend of mine in Chicago has the most soothing house I've ever visited. The minute you walk into the place, you hear a lovely trickle of water from a fountain on the sun-porch; it sounds like a calming musical instrument. I was so instantly soothed the moment I first heard this sound that my immediate reaction was to ask, "Where do I buy a fountain for my home?" Sure, this wasn't the same as a day on the beach listening to the ocean waves or an afternoon spent skipping stones over a glassy pond, but let me just tell you that the gentle rush of water from that fountain came very, very close to the feeling I get from these experiences.

My friend just laughed and directed me to the garden center where he'd bought his little stress buster. I could only imagine coming home from a long road trip or a busy day at the office and finding instant happiness and calmness thanks to the sound of a little trickling H_2O.

The same friend also had the Geek Squad wire his entire house so that gentle, almost New Age music could be heard in every room. Was I at a friend's house or a five-star spa? Imagine the trickling water plus the sound of a harp and flute. In a nanosecond, I was eying a very comfy-looking lounge chair and wondering if he would notice if I took a little nap.

There was just something about this house that was totally relaxing and that made me feel like my house . . . was not. When I walked into my house, I noted that there was no fountain, no sweet music to greet me or chill me out while I did the dishes or took a shower. I could only imagine that music in my bedroom while I was reading a good book or writing a few notes. Heaven!

The point here is simple: You need to make *su casa* the most relaxing home base possible because it really is your refuge. Yes, it's fun to spend money on vacations and great clothes, but what's more important is making your home your haven—one that's available to you every single day. Even on a stressful day, you will know that you can always retreat to your own little refuge.

I did a little investigating to find out ways to soothe your residence. It doesn't matter if your home is 900 square feet or a mansion. I've tried the following techniques in my Cleveland house and even in my office, and they were really transformative for my mood.

get rid of the clutter

While I don't think of myself as a clutter king, I have to admit that I can get a little bit messy. I would never leave food on a plate in the middle of my bedroom or even in a hotel room. But I will rip through a pile of clothes, making it look like a strong wind just blew through the room. Call me "Hurricane Jim." My singing partner and great friend Anne Cochran teases me all the time when we're on tour.

"When I go into Jim's hotel room, he can be there only one minute and suddenly his stuff is *everywhere*," she says. "Only Jim can have stuff on the floor and in the sink before most people even unzip their suitcase."

I wish I could argue with Anne, but she's absolutely right: I like to spread out and unpack quickly. In my own defense, I'm usually going through my stuff with an eye to the next event or the next day. I'm just trying to reorganize so I only need carry-ons. But if you catch me at the wrong point in this process, it looks like a big mess. (I swear that I quickly clean it up and everything is back in the cases.) If I know my flight is at the crack of dawn, I'll unpack my suitcase and repack it with just what I need on top, so the morning goes smoothly and I don't have to fish around for that blue shirt.

common scents at home

Stop for a moment and take a deep breath if you're home. How does your home smell? Does it smell like last night's

(continued on page 38)

soothe expert:

Amelia Love Hatcher
on Clutter

When it comes to decluttering, I have to defer to the experts. One such guru on the topic is the Clutter Queen, aka Amelia Love Hatcher. Here are her tips for purging clutter and finding space.

LEARN WHAT YOUR "STUFF" MEANS

Clutter can tear families apart. I grew up in a family where my grandmother was borderline hoarder. My grandmother had a stroke and then a horrible fall at home and was placed in a nursing home. She had zero affairs in order, and my family had a few weeks to remove 60 years of stuff. It really did stress us out as a family. Then I told them that the word *stuff* breaks down this way:

- S is for stress. Stuff stresses us out and can be exhausting.
- T is for the time it takes to go through all the piles.
- U is for unfinished stuff you will get to one day.
- F is for fatigue because stuff makes us tired. It takes energy to move things around over and over again.
- F is for free because you can set your mind, body, and soul free by decluttering and removing the stuff from your life.

DECLUTTER FOR YOUR HEALTH

Clutter is stressing everyone out because we lead overwhelming lives, and having too much stuff just makes it that much more overwhelming. Doctors say that a cluttered environment keeps our thoughts cluttered. It has a negative impact on both adults and children.

CREATE A DECLUTTERING SYSTEM

If I came into your home and asked you to locate a few things such as your birth certificate, the title to your car, or a hammer, could you find them immediately? Or would you need some time to search, dig, and then stress because you still couldn't find what you needed? I help people put a system in place so they can find each and every thing. I call it the spoon effect. I bet if I asked you to find me a spoon, you could go straight to it. You put your spoons in the same drawer, use them, wash them, and then replace them. That rule can work all over your home. It's creating a great habit that works for you and then you stick with it. A little movin' and shakin' of the stuff, and you're suddenly feeling better!

START SMALL

What I try to get people to do is pick one task. You don't want to tackle an entire closet as a whole. Start with something simple like shoes. You just start dividing them by color or style. Then I go over the rules. If you didn't wear them last summer, you won't put them on this summer. Get rid of them! By starting with a category such as belts or shoes, you're not overwhelming yourself. If there is one zone of your closet that's bugging you, then stay out of that zone until the end. You can even load a laundry basket with the bug-zone items. After you sort and purge, reload everything back into your nice new space.

DIVIDE AND CONQUER

Divide everything into trash, giveaways/donations, or keepers. It's just that easy. As for the piles, don't leave them in the closet, or you will end up putting everything back. Put trash in the trash and things to be given

away or donated in the trunk of your car. Get these out of the space and then out of your home so they will leave for good. Then go back into the closet and start with something else: handbags, men's ties, and clothing by seasons. Grab all your long-sleeve shirts and go through them, then move to the next category. Just do this one thing at a time.

MANAGE MULTIPLES

Do you have multiples of items? Take out everything that's similar or in the same family, such as all the short-sleeve shirts or the black sweaters. Place them side by side and you will be able to decide easily what you're really fond of and what's faded and needs to be removed and given to Goodwill. Before you know it, you will weed things out. Put a number on how many of each item you will keep. Then when you do buy another black V-neck, you must purge an old one. You have to purge when you buy or you're creating clutter.

DITCH THE SKINNY JEANS

People will say, "I'm going on a diet." I believe that you possibly will go on a diet. If those skinny jeans have been in your closet for three years and you get back to that size in a few weeks, those jeans will be outdated. When you're back to your desired size, buy new clothes. Make that your goal: You will hit Target or Neiman Marcus when you achieve your goal.

SAVE MEMENTOS—NOT JUNK

If it's that first-kiss shirt or a favorite college tee, then get it out of your closet and put it in a plastic box. Label the box *Memories*. Your kids are not going to appreciate that hole-filled sweatshirt someday. They will be saying, "Why would my mother keep this?" I had an elderly client who

lost her husband and kept his favorite pair of jeans. She said, "All I have now is that pair of jeans." Yes, you should have keepsakes. But do something with them. One way was to make some small throw pillows out of his favorite flannel shirt and denim. She could see them on her bed each day without them taking up too much space. For instance, I kept my mother's recipe cards, her favorite apron, and the wooden spoon she stirred so many of our favorite meals with and put them in a shadow box. Now I can see and enjoy these things, including her precious handwriting, each time I go into my kitchen. I do advise you not to keep boxes and boxes of someone else's clothing. Instead, keep that cute pillow he or she loved, but don't cram it in your closet. Keep it in your memory box or display it for comfort. Place the priceless items in a shadow box to enjoy them in a sweet space. If you've lost a loved one and you're not sure what to get rid of, then box it up and look at again in six months. That time might give you clarity that you just don't have right now.

TACKLE THE JEWELRY BOX

Lay a large blanket or towel of a solid color across your bed. Dump that jewelry box and start sorting. Sort by color and style—for example, silver or gold, dressy or casual. Pick your favorites. Do you really need 15 pairs of red earrings when you lean toward silver and gold? Think about your wardrobe. Think about what's heavy and hurts to wear. Let these go. Keep that favorite jewelry and toss the ones that just junk up your drawer. If your mother-in-law gave you a piece of jewelry and you're guilt-keeping it, then box it up and get it out of your way. Don't let unwanted things clutter your mind and home because you feel bad. Stick them in that memory box or in that no-guilt Goodwill bag. It's your life to live—do it clutter free and organized.

overly garlicked spaghetti dish? Or does it smell like the dog just ran in after playing in the sprinklers? Maybe your house smells like that dirty laundry you've wanted to get to all week. I don't know about you, but smells that remind me of home chores (doing laundry, taking out the trash, cleaning the bathroom) make me feel rather tense. Perhaps it's been a long day and I don't have the mental bandwidth to add a chore to my list of things to do once I get home. The smell just reminds me of how little time I have to take care of things.

Hello, rising anxiety levels!

My friend's house with the fountain also smells amazing (of course); I feel as if I have just walked into a bakery. Each room has the scent of vanilla, like cupcakes fresh out of the oven. The vanilla smell immediately fills my nostrils and reminds me of the days when my mom baked me something after school. As I wander around and sniff this sweet scent, my sense of relaxation just deepens. I read a study by the Smell and Taste Treatment and Research Foundation in Chicago. It basically told the world that if someone wants to seduce a man, the key isn't some flowery perfume or one of those musky smells. Instead, the smell of freshly baked cinnamon buns was the most appealing to men. Again, it's the vanilla! (PS: The study also found that the smell of grapefruit—on you or in your house—made people believe you were younger by almost a decade. Food for thought! Perhaps I could have most of my house smell like vanilla, but my bathroom smell like grapefruit so I will begin to think I am younger!)

Another way to use scents to create a sanctuary is with sprays or essential oils, which you can tote along with you anywhere you go. I bought an amazing spearmint-eucalyptus linen spray that I'm addicted to these days. Believe me when I say that I take it everywhere. When I'm on the road, it's so nice to smell that familiar scent and breathe in some calm. You can bring your favorite scent with you in the car, at the office, or on a trip.

The key to soothing with scent is simple:

○ **Get rid of any nasty smells in your house— ASAP!** Yes, this might require a deep cleaning and some regular trash and laundry removal, but it's worth it in the long run. Anything that smells funky should be chucked in the trash, and then immediately deposited in the bin outside to be taken away. Open a window for fresh air.

○ **Invest in some great candles or room sprays.** They're not just an indulgence, but are also good for your mental health. I'm really partial to the smell of, again, vanilla or linen, which makes even a winter day smell like spring.

○ **Remember to actually light the candles.** A lot of us have candles around, but they're more like props because we never fire them up. Light them when you're home and enjoy them—just make sure to put them out! I light candles each night when I read at home or even watch TV. It's a wonderful, relaxing ritual.

start the day with great music

Now that most of us have smartphones, it's easy to wake up in your own personal spa with an alarm that plays soothing music. But why isolate the tranquility produced by great music to that initial moment in your day when you're still half asleep? Someone once gave me a great suggestion that I still use today: Set your alarm to let beautiful music fill your house at different times throughout the day. For instance, why should that last 10 minutes you have at home before you rush out the door for work be a totally frazzled experience? Why not set a timer and have a beautiful song usher you out the door? Why not make sure your phone goes off with soothing sounds during that walk to the bus or when you're in the tub every night? And by beautiful, I mean *your* kind of beautiful. If Metallica does it for you, then crank it up. Classical? Why not? It's a personal choice, but I do know there is nothing better than having your favorite music around you all the time. The point is to add music to the times in your life that you know are stressful to bring down the frantic quality of the moment.

Find some of my favorite soothing songs for my own personal "rush hour" moments at SootheYourWorld.com.

soothe now

When was the last time you listened to your favorite song or artist? If you can't remember, make it a weekend project to fill your phone with music so that you'll enjoy it on a regular basis.

set up your inner sanctum

Have you ever noticed that when you walk into a spa, you feel the tension begin to melt away before you even have a treatment? You're likely being cloaked in a preplanned double whammy of beautiful music and calming scents upon entering. But there is actually much more at work here, because spas make sure that their entry points are designed to make you leave your regular life literally at the door.

In other words, it's all about the entry point, your door to stress relief. Mike McAdams, who is a co-owner and the designer of the ultra glamorous Lake Austin Spa Resort in Austin, Texas, reports that spas use many different sensory cues to make sure the nervous energy and troubles from outside stay there.

How can you incorporate what a spa does when it comes to your own home?

Start by focusing on the entrance to your home. Of course many of us who live in apartments or have small homes can't exactly build a flowering pathway to the front door. Perhaps you can't have an archway with roses blooming overhead or the perfect Japanese rock garden as your bridge between the stress of the outside world and your home. But you can look at the entrance of your home and make a few great changes. This might include a hanging plant or a fancy, colorful welcome mat. Or maybe you could buy a few big pots and plant seasonal flowers or other foliage at your door—a grouping of Shasta daisies in the summer, a big pot of marigolds in the fall. Ideally the flowers should be in soothing colors such as pale yellow, lilac, and pale pink.

Nix clutter. Do you have clutter leading the way from your car to your door? This is common when people have to go through their garage in order to get into the house. You need to clean up the area. Again, the last thing you need to see is your home in shambles the minute you pull up. A few tips:

- **Designate an area for keeping all your athletic equipment.** You don't need to wade through a sea of bikes and balls to reach the front door.
- **Have a major garage-cleaning day.** Everything that's not in a cabinet or put away in a box or plastic container must go.
- **Consider renting a storage facility as a way to reduce the anxiety of seeing all this clutter.** Or if you truly have too much stuff, and have a backyard, you can look into getting a shed.
- **Think about painting the garage interior a calming color like yellow and sealing the floor for easy cleaning.** Imagine pulling into an organized garage that looks clean and polished.

Suddenly, home becomes more of an oasis than a form of a giant to-do list.

Clean up your dump area. Many of us step inside and go right to "the dump": that table, chair, or special stair that gets to hold your mail, the newspaper, a briefcase or computer case, a purse, and that empty Tupperware salad container you used at lunch. Sure, sure, you're just using this spot as a pit stop, and you'll clean it up once you make sure everyone is home and alive. Stop in the name of soothing! And put your shoes back on your feet. Clean up that dump area (or don't create one in the first place). With that area, you indicate that the minute you walk into your home, there should be chaos. "That chaos creates an immediate sense of being overwhelmed and buried by your life," says Anne McCall Wilson, former vice-president of Spas, Fairmont Raffles Hotels International, and now a principal for McCall and Wilson.

A quick fix-it tip: Have one basket for all the junk. It should be cleaned out daily, and set inside a closet so you don't have to look at it piling up. It shouldn't be a huge basket either, as you are not starting a Goodwill collection here, but instead are just putting a few things in limbo while you tend to your life. You have to clean out the basket before it overflows, which will keep you disciplined. And this routine also helps you not to trip over a zillion things and fall down the stairs.

Invest in mood-enhancing lighting that is not too bright or too dark. Don't go for a big light overhead, but instead choose a smaller one that casts a subtle glow. You want your home to look warm and welcoming, not like you're walking into the DMV. Set a dimmer switch timer to keep your light dim when you return at night, but make it a bit brighter for the day.

Remind you of . . . you. If you have the room, buy a small table for your entryway and place framed pictures of great vacations or beloved family members on the table. You want to have a clear line between work and home. Home should remind you of loved ones and special times.

how to come home

I know this sounds crazy, but how you enter the house often reflects how you feel about coming home. Counselors say that you should give yourself several moments to unwind when you first enter the door. Maybe as a family you agree that everyone should make an effort not to rush and create stress the minute the door opens. Unless the house is burning down or someone is bleeding, everyone can make time for a simple hello and five minutes of quiet to let you get your head straight and not dread walking in the door. Likewise, you will also have to agree not to open the door and start shouting, "Who made this mess? Did you do your homework? What is that smell?"

If you say a gentle hello to your partner and other family members, they will calm down and perhaps not give you a laundry list of complaints and things to do before you even take off your coat. Remind those who live with you that you need to ease into the next situation. Can they just give you 5 to 10 minutes to unwind and get acclimated before launching into the inevitable to-do list?

Other ways to soothe your home:

○ **Get rid of the fake flowers and invest in some real ones.** You can buy them cheaply at the grocery store, and they really do add a lot to the room.

○ **Buy quality, foot-friendly rugs if you have hardwood floors.** There's something very soothing about the contrast between the hardness of wood and the softness of rugs.

○ **Rethink your kitchen.** Most of us spend so much time in the kitchen, yet it's usually the most chaotic room in the house. Take a moment to walk into your own kitchen. What do you see? Clutter? Mess? A zillion papers from school and work everywhere? Get rid of half of what's on your counters and surfaces. How do you feel now? Also think about taking the TV out of the kitchen because of the noise factor. Replace it with a stereo or an iHome for soothing tunes while you cook.

○ **Make a list.** You can do this on paper or on your phone. There is something satisfying about checking things off that you really didn't want to do but did. You'll feel so much better once the garage is clean or the junk drawer is organized—a weight will be lifted from your shoulders.

○ **Rethink the rooms in your house that you never use.** Maybe it's a living room that goes unused because you do your living in a great room. Or you never eat in the formal dining room except on Thanksgiving Day. Looking at unused rooms is a huge stressor, studies indicate. Why? Your brain is trained to fill up spaces, so now you're thinking that you need a piece of furniture that you can't afford or locate. All of this equals stress because suddenly you have another item on your to-do list. Rethink how you can use the room to your advantage. Make sure each room in your home is functional. What would you do with some dream space? Clear out your unused space and you can live that dream. Get rid of that home gym that's gathering dust and make it into a playroom or an office. That dining room could become a great reading room, with an overstuffed chaise lounge. You can create your own Pilates studio out of that back room where you just dump extra clothes. What could you do with some dream space? Clear out your unused space and you can live that dream.

○ **Let there be light.** If your house has dark areas without any windows, add lighting and mirrors to bounce the light. If rooms with windows are too dark, consider getting rid of those heavy drapes and putting up shutters or gauzy curtains. Your brain feels soothed by seeing the light, since a dark room can be depressing.

soothe now

Remember that your environment is a reflection of your life. If your house looks chaotic, you will feel chaotic. A calm demeanor results from a clutter-free, clean, inviting home.

○ **Think comfort.** Sure, the couch that looks like it belongs on an episode of *Mad Men* is pretty sexy, but if it kills your back when you test it in the store, pass on buying it. You want your rest spaces to be comfortable and inviting. Make sure that you have more than one rest space. It's not enough to have only that leather chair. Each room should have a piece of furniture people just want to sink into and stay. Don't make it a case where everyone in your family fights over the one great spot. Comfort versus style? I'll go for comfort every time.

○ **Your bedroom is your *everything*.** We'll talk about this more in Chapter 4, but don't cheap out on anything that goes into your bedroom. Yes, buy those 500-thread-count sheets when they go on sale, and spend a few extra bucks on your bed. Invest in good pillows. Sleep is when you really de-stress and restore. You can't afford to have a nonrestful rest area.

○ **Decorate your bedroom to soothe.** Use neutral, calming colors and make your bed. An unmade bed is distracting. Put fresh flowers on your bedside table.

soothe expert:

Tisha Morris on Feng Shui

Tisha Morris knows about having a Zen home. The feng shui expert promises to transform your life one room at a time.

"I want to help make your home a sanctuary. Your space should support you and not challenge you," says Tisha. "The best part of making these changes is that your living space will bring about desired changes in your life—whether it is your career, life purpose, relationships, or money."

What is feng shui? Some might think it's a bit woo-woo or too rule-oriented, but Tisha has a commonsense approach to the art of arranging your personal space and making the energy of it work for you. She also considers herself a "home whisperer" and "space healer."

"I clear and balance the energy in spaces, and as a result, you can expect sweeping changes in your life," she says. Here are her tips for transforming your space and life with feng shui.

START WITH A CLEAN SLATE

You can have the most perfect feng shui plan, but if there is clutter around your house, it will defeat all your efforts. I define clutter as something that is no longer in your best interests to have around, and it takes up space that could be used for something else. Nice clean space is key in your home and office.

Why is having a clean and clear space key? You want that yin and yang balance from quiet space. Too much stuff around our homes with no space makes us feel stressed and claustrophobic. It's like the walls are closing in. You might think it's good to have all these life mementos around, but a lot of it is just clutter. If you feel stressed in your own home or stuck in your life for any reason, it's time to de-clutter.

TACKLE A SMALL SPACE FIRST

I always tell people to start with the easiest space first. It will get the
ball rolling. It might be your clothes closet. Get rid of items that are
easy to get rid of and that you don't have to think twice about throwing
out or donating. You know you're never wearing that dress or suit
again, so give it away. Get the energy moving. Once the energy
moves, it will give you the momentum to throw away other things and
work on the other rooms.

Everyone has his or her own Achilles' heel. For some, there are
papers everywhere. For others, it's clothes, jewelry, family heirlooms,
and inherited items that might be a little sentimental, but frankly you
have no idea what to do with them. You know what should go—and it
should actually go *now*.

DEAL WITH HEIRLOOMS

Many people have inherited things from their parents or perhaps are
empty nesters who are hanging on to their kid's belongings. Literally,
both groups feel like they don't have an inch of space. They're anxious
in their own homes and feel like the walls are closing in. Of course,
with inherited items, there is an element of respect and love. But if you
really feel that couch or that big dresser doesn't belong in your house,
you might want to donate it to a charity your parents loved. In this way,
you're moving the piece with respect and finding the best loving home
for it. Those who have passed on really don't care anymore about that
one knickknack or that ugly old chair. Give it away if you don't really
want it.

DON'T HIDE YOUR CLUTTER—EXPEL IT

Don't think that shoving your clutter in a closet or under your bed will cleanse your home or your mind. Your subconscious mind will still know it's there. It's not emotionally cleansing to just relocate items to another spot in your own home. You're working on emotion clearing here, and to do that you must get rid of stuff. It's very freeing. You're getting rid of items that you bought during a certain period in your life. You might still associate them with that specific time. But that was then, and this is now. It's an emotional breakthrough to get rid of it and move on.

CREATE AN OASIS

It's fine to carve out a space for your TV, but also make a great space to sit and read a book or listen to music. TV is chaotic energy. Why not plan a great relaxation spot to sit and read and listen to soft piano playing. Nothing kills the soothing element of a room like a blaring TV.

BRING THE OUTDOORS IN

Living plants are fantastic. You want to incorporate natural plants and air into your house. I suggest an air purifier for every house. NASA did a study, however, that said having one plant in your home is the equivalent of having one air purifier. I always make sure to have a plant in the kitchen to absorb the toxic gas fumes. Having a plant in the bedroom is great feng shui because it cleanses your aura field while you sleep.

USE MIRRORS STRATEGICALLY

Mirrors serve a lot of different functions in a home, including stimulating energy in spots where you need more energy, such as a dark hallway or in a room with no windows. You don't want to use mirrors in an area like your bedroom, where rest and relaxation are key. Remember that mirrors are energetic, which is the opposite of soothing. You also want to be careful of what the mirror reflects. Don't have your mirror reflect a dresser top filled with clutter. That just doubles the chaos. You do want to have a mirror reflecting a beautiful plant.

HARNESS THE POWER OF COLOR

Monotones and neutrals are good for people who have a lot of anxiety. Other good colors are blue and green, which are cool colors on the color wheel. I'd always avoid primary colors if you want to soothe—especially in children's rooms. As a society, we think kids' rooms should be bright and painted vibrant red and yellow. Wrong! When you paint little Timmy's room hot purple and put jungle animals all over the wall, it's no wonder he can't sleep and his teacher thinks he has attention deficit disorder. Calming colors are always the way to go because you want your home to be your refuge from the world.

A great feng shui way would be to paint the master bedroom in a warm chocolate color. You can use dark tones that have a nice, romantic flair to them. This warms up the room and makes it your own personal sanctuary. Try a dark burgundy if you want more yin and a more tranquil rest. Also, always have dimmers in the bedroom. It's good to keep a lower light in there.

EMBRACE INDIVIDUAL SPACE

I recommend that you agree upon shared spaces, but also each have an individual space in your home. Perhaps each of you can have the luxury of separate offices. Decorate your own space however you please. If you don't have the luxury of having two private spaces, then just have a spot in the house that is yours and off limits to everyone else. It can be a little cove in a corner or even just a shelf or a counter that belongs to you alone. It could be a space that's very small and you just have one chair in it to meditate. Or the bathtub could be yours because he showers in the other bathroom. It's essential to have some quiet space that is your own. Once you get into that space, you're able to settle in and get quiet. Remember to make your space beautiful with nice, calming candles and plants. And just as with any other space in the house, you will make sure that there is no clutter. Keep the energy fresh. Don't allow stuff to just sit there.

ENERGIZE YOUR HOME

If you feel like your house is full of dead energy, take action. Declutter. Move the furniture around. Use sage to get rid of dead energy. I've developed a smudge spray for this purpose, or you could use rose water. My spray clears the energy because it contains rose water, sage, and cedarwood. Your goal is to leave a high vibration. I promise that you can actually feel the energy in your home shift after you clear the dead energy out.

4

soothe yourself to sleep

A re you getting your z's? It turns out that sleep, or lack of it, is a key factor to staying calm, cool, and collected all day.

Luckily I'm not someone who suffers from insomnia except if I eat too close to when I go to bed or drink a little too much wine. As for my sleep routine, if I'm home in Cleveland, I'm in luck because I've designed my bedroom as a retreat. We're talking dim lights, not some big overhead searchlight. Friends like to give me candles, so I set them up in the bedroom. I'm not a fan of big fluffy white comforters, but instead like a few good blankets that you can pull on or toss off depending on the crazy Midwestern temperatures.

Just like most of you out there, I didn't really want to spend the money, but I convinced myself to buy good pillows. (You can wait for pillows to go on sale at department stores.) These pillows are something I use every single night of my life (at least when I'm home), which made this purchase different from buying a new shirt. I spend a lot of time with these pillows, and I wanted to invest in my relaxation each and every night. My bedroom is really comfortable, truly a place to escape from it all.

I know that sleep routines are popular these days, as are elaborate getting-ready-for-sleep to-do lists that some people follow rigidly. I like to drink a little mint herbal tea at night and will usually have something sweet, like dark chocolate almonds. On cold winter nights in Cleveland, I'll watch a little TV in my den before turning in or talk on the phone with friends or family. It's nice to end the day with a friendly voice.

The problem for me is that I'm overstimulated by performing and am used to activity all around me. My mom is like that too in that she can't sit still. At night, I'll talk on the phone, walk around the house, and check for messages. Yet about an hour before it's time to sleep, I force myself to actually wind it down, or I would never be able to drift off. Of course, when I'm on tour, there are times when I go from a show to my hotel room completely wound up. Those are the nights when it's really tough to relax, especially when I know that I have to be up at the crack of dawn to catch a plane or do a morning radio show. I'm sure you experience those moments when you turn off the lights or the television and your body is exhausted, but your mind is still racing. What do you do to get proper rest? This was a question for the experts.

are you fatigued?

The sad thing is that a lot of us go to bed at a reasonable time intending to get our eight hours of unbroken sleep. But despite our best intentions, we can't drift off. Is it good enough simply to close your eyes and rest? It turns out that the answer is no. If you're anxious when your head hits the pillow, you're actually waking up your brain by your thoughts, says psychologist Stephanie Silberman, PhD, a fellow of the American Academy of Sleep Medicine and the author of *The Insomnia Workbook*.

I don't want to make you even more anxious, but if you spend too many nights not really sleeping and just "resting," not only will you be tired, but you will also hurt your ability to remember things while becoming quite moody and worked up in general. Dr. Silberman has a great tip, among many others, concerning how to calm your mind. The next time you can't drift off, practice her "thought stopping" process. To do so, just visualize an actual stop sign each time you start to experience any anxious thoughts. You put up the stop sign; obey it and thus shut down your thoughts.

your brain and sleep

Before we get to more tips, I have one more reason why you're extra grumpy (and stressed) when you don't sleep enough. Studies show that sleep loss is actually bad for your health in

soothe now

Another favorite from Silberman is called Progressive Muscle Relaxation.

To do this, first lie down in a comfortable position on your back. Then:

- Start at your toes and tighten the muscles there.
- Hold for five seconds. Release.
- Continue with each muscle group, traveling up the length of your entire body. Practice breathing in through your nose and out through your mouth during this process.

You should feel relaxed by the time you reach your head and neck.

several ways. Scientists know that lack of sleep can measurably decrease your cognitive functions while also reducing the speed at which you process information and your attention to detail.

So let's say you're not sleeping well. You overcaffeinate yourself just to stay awake at your job and get through your morning deadlines. Now you're adding caffeine into the situation, which means that you're stressing out your system while making yourself jumpy. No wonder you just grabbed three brownies off the tray at work. Nothing goes with coffee like a little—no, make that a lot of—sugar. The good news is that once you start sleeping again, you will actually make better decisions and avoid all of the above. The moral of the story: Get your seven to nine hours of solid uninterrupted sleep in order to have all-day natural energy that doesn't depend on stimulants like caffeine or sugar.

prepare to lull yourself to sleep

Perhaps you're freaked out because it's the end of the month and the bills are due (again). Or there's that problem person from work, whose words keep echoing in your mind. Maybe you decided to watch an action movie before bedtime and your mind is just too amped up to allow you to sleep. If you're overwrought or overstimulated, the mere idea of getting seven to nine hours of unbroken sleep—your goal as an adult, say researchers—might seem like a pipe dream.

Even when your eyelids feel heavy and your body seems relaxed, it's still difficult to drift off to la-la land. The worst is when you're having trouble going to sleep and you keep checking the LED clock to see how much time has passed since you realized that you better get to sleep . . . although you're still awake. Just glancing at that blue-green LED light is doing exactly what you don't want here, which is telling your brain to wake up. Research shows that anything electronic is stimulating.

There are several ways you can beat this nightly stress routine.

Plan your wind-down time. Shelby Freedman Harris, PsyD, director of the Behavioral Sleep Medicine Program at the Sleep-Wake Disorders Center at Montefiore Medical

Center, says that you need to plan for sleep a good 30 to 45 minutes before you ever pull back the covers. "Keep a general schedule for that wind-down hour so your body and your mind start to know you're closer to bedtime," she advises.

Stop doing anything that stimulates your brain—such as jumping on your computer or even on your cell phone to text friends—for 30 to 45 minutes before sleep. Scientists agree that the blue-green light of electronics actually stimulates your brain into awake mode. This means that working before you go to bed or answering e-mails is a great way to ensure that you're going to have a sleepless night.

Many people are trained to watch TV before bedtime, though most experts agree this isn't a smart move. I'm guilty of watching a little TV, but I'm trying to read instead. I do find it's easier to fall asleep if I don't watch TV. In the end, most agree that it's okay to watch a little TV at bedtime, but nothing that's too exciting and stimulating. You shouldn't watch the depressing world news or a violent action movie, but you can watch a *Seinfeld* or *Everybody Loves Raymond* episode for a nice chuckle before closing your eyes. In other words, avoid media that makes you anxious in any way.

Give yourself some zen before bed. Prayer before bed is actually a great way to calm your mind and talk to a higher authority before you zone out. I've also learned that a simple meditation done before you go to sleep also does wonders. This doesn't have to be you sitting in the middle of the bed chanting Om while your partner and dog stare at you. You can simply sit comfortably in a chair or on the bed with your eyes closed and do a little deep breathing before you retire.

You're sending out a signal to your body that you're transitioning between the stress of your day or even the juggling act of your night (doing laundry, laying out clothes for the morning) and a more relaxing time that's all about you: sleep.

Dunk it. I don't mean play basketball or grab some cookies and milk, which is a high-calorie, sugary way to end the day. Instead, it is helpful to jump into a soothingly hot bath at the end of the day. This is an age-old way to relax. Your body will melt into that tub, and you can allow your daily worries to flow into the water. Just sitting in hot water actually raises your core body temperature, which helps you feel drowsy. And if you add a soothing scent like vanilla or lavender to the bath, then you're really setting yourself up for some nice sleep.

Tea for you. I knew my tea habit was a great way to nod off, and scientifically it's actually perfect. According to the National Center for Complementary and Alternative Medicine, chamomile tea is good for reducing anxiety and insomnia. In addition, the warmth of herbal tea at bedtime triggers a sleepy feeling, and when a cup of a warm beverage becomes a nightly ritual, it signals your body to calm down. I drink chamomile tea, which has even been called a surefire sleep aid. Studies show that chamomile has anti-anxiety effects, although these studies are not yet conclusive. Chamomile does feature apigenin, a flavonoid that contributes to relaxing. Avoid any caffeinated tea and opt to brew chamomile tea or any other herbal tea of your choice. Nix sugar or sugary creamers, since they'll work against the relaxation you're craving.

(continued on page 62)

soothe expert:

Dr. Drew Ramsey on Sleep

I went to *Soothe* expert Dr. Drew Ramsey for his thoughts on sleep and curing insomnia. Here are his tips.

EASE INTO SLEEP

You have to think of your brain as if it's a baby. I have a six-month-old and a three-year-old. I don't just toss them into bed and say, "Okay, sleep now!" As adults, we expect to have this harried evening routine and then just switch our brains into sleep mode. It doesn't work that way.

USE LIGHT STRATEGICALLY

Our brains are wired to detect light, and the hormones that put our brains to sleep are wired to respond to a lack of light. We are supposed to get up with the sun and calm down when the sun goes down. I know that's not always possible with our busy schedules, but it's helpful to dim the lights at night to mimic our natural tendency. You don't want to be around really bright lights and then tell your brain to go to sleep. I have dimmer switches on all my lights. At seven at night, all the lights in the house go down. We even eat dinner by candlelight, which is romantic. And I don't have a TV in my house.

DEVELOP YOUR SLEEP ROUTINE

You need to have an evening routine. At my house, we eat a healthy meal together and have a bath. All the lights in the entire house go down at dinner and afterward. Then we have some nonstimulating entertainment like reading a book. Adults can do the same routine to make sure they don't overstimulate themselves at night.

STEER CLEAR OF STIMULANTS

Avoid caffeine and alcohol before bedtime. People have a few drinks, then can't sleep because they're stimulated. Also, anything with a screen—TV, computer, tablet—is stimulating. Even if you can fall asleep after looking at electronics, the light from the screen might be preventing good quality sleep.

BEAT INSOMNIA

If you are having trouble falling asleep, get out of bed. I ask people to do some simple yoga with deep breathing. On a rug near your bed, do a child's pose or a downward-facing dog. We're talking really easy stuff while doing deep, cleansing breaths to clear your mind of any anxiety. You're giving yourself permission here not to deal with any worries. You have a pressing deadline. You have bills that are due. You can't fall asleep because you're worried. Give yourself permission to rest. You're not dismissing your worries. You're just taking a break from them to get your needed sleep. My wife will say to me, "Drew, it's midnight. You've been writing for four hours. It's time to rest. You can worry about that deadline tomorrow." It's permission to put everything aside and just focus on sleep.

TRY A NATURAL SLEEP AID

Many doctors recommend melatonin, which is a safe natural hormone that puts your brain to sleep. I've used it when I've had trouble sleeping, although I'd rather use herbal teas 45 minutes before the desired bedtime. I also like valerian root, which I put in my nighttime tea to relax. It's up to each person to experiment with what makes him or her sleepy, and to rely on your doctor's advice as to what's safe and natural. With a doctor's permission and common sense, you can explore melatonin or other options.

MAKE SLEEP A PRIORITY

If your sleep is off-kilter, it needs to be your number one priority in life. You need to retrain your body to sleep. Make a schedule of what you will do. Dim the lights. Have your tea. Do some light stretching. With the lights low, brush your teeth and get into bed. Another helpful tip is to really exhaust your body during the day. Leave work at 6:00 p.m. and go to the gym and work out hard until 7:00 p.m. Then have that nice meal and read a book or watch some nonstimulating TV. But at 10:00 p.m., really start the major wind-down. All screens are off. You take a hot bath. For all of you attached to your e-mails, ask yourself, "Is my in-box more important than my health?" Nothing is a bigger priority than your need for sleep. Think of this fact: If you don't sleep for three days, you can become psychotic. Make sleep your mission.

Check out. Dr. Michael Breus, aka the Sleep Doctor, recommends this nighttime practice: Picture yourself on vacation at the most relaxing spot in your world. Maybe it's on a white sandy beach or at a ski retreat in the mountains. Maybe you will imagine yourself swinging gently on a sun-faded hammock set up especially for you in breezy, lush Hawaii on that empty beach where the sound of soft ocean waves fills your ears. Hear the sound of the surf crashing and feel the light mist of water. Your brain is a powerful instrument, and the simple suggestion of relaxation can instantly soothe you. This is also a great technique for stressful daily moments. When you can steal away for a moment and close your eyes, picture that vacation you will take . . . someday.

Smell the relaxation. If you have trouble falling asleep, it's helpful to keep some sleep-inducing scents available in your bedroom. The best include lavender, chamomile, geranium, and rose. My favorite is lavender, and I order my scents from a mom-and-pop store called Magnolia Scents in Independence, Kansas, because they make their own lavender-vanilla combination scent that you can spray into the air. I even spray it on my pillows when I travel.

try a little meditation

Okay, Dr. Drew has busted me for e-mailing before bedtime, when I should be ramping up my efforts to get some shut-eye. (Note to self: Do not e-mail Dr. Drew after 10:00 p.m.) The idea of meditating before bed intrigued me, so I asked the experts for a few simple exercises to do before bedtime.

Breathe: Breathe deeply from your abdomen while listening to soft music. Focus on how your breath goes in and out. You can do this lying down in bed, with your hands resting lightly on your stomach.

Imagine: This is like the "check out" vacation scenario on page 61. Imagine a place that soothes you. It could be a lovely park bench or your grandmother's kitchen table. What you choose is up to you. The idea is to transport your mind to a place of joy and safety. Imagine that scene for several minutes, focusing on the details of it. How does it feel? Smell? Look? You should naturally relax just thinking about it.

Meditate: Take several minutes before bed to just sit and calm your mind. If that's hard for you, then keep a journal and write your daily worries in it before bedtime. Leave space after each worry to write about how you will solve the issue. Once you close the journal, turn the lights off and sit on the end of your bed or lie down on it. Breathe deeply and focus on calming your mind through simple meditation. You don't have to say *Om* and sit with your legs crossed. Just calm down your mind and use a mental broom to sweep away invading thoughts that are worrisome.

get on schedule

If at all possible, you need to get on a sleep schedule. I'm not someone who likes to sleep too late, but I have plenty of musician friends who can sleep until 2:00 p.m. after a gig the night before. The key is to never oversleep, because it throws off your patterns or worse. According to a study from the Université Laval in Quebec, Canada, those who oversleep have a higher risk of type 2 diabetes, obesity, and back problems.

soothe now

Say no to naps. I know this one is depressing, but all the experts say that if you lose a little sleep the night before, don't make it up with a daily nap. Again, that just messes up your body's internal sleep clock, plus napping doesn't give us the restorative, healing powers of a night of unbroken sleep. Keep yourself awake and go to bed at the normal time that night.

Just sleeping in for a few days resets your body clock. Stick to a routine to make sure you're sleepy at the same time each night. Of course there will be life events that throw off your best sleep plans. Just get back on track the next night and resume your routine.

Go beyond counting sheep and find more great tips to soothe yourself to sleep at SootheYourWorld.com.

soothe sleep recap

I know we just covered a lot of sleep techniques, so here's a recap of what you should do to soothe before bedtime:

- Create a routine. For me it's TV, tea, and reading before bed. I've trained my brain to know that the next step is sleep. Bedtime routines tell your mind that the day is coming to an end.
- Write down your worries. Remember that once you put your fears down on paper, you will give yourself permission to take time off from facing them until morning. Remind yourself that nothing can be solved now. Your only task is sleep.
- Work with the light. Set dimmer switches to remind your brain that the evening is coming to an end. Don't shock yourself with bright bathroom light when you brush your teeth. Keep the lights low all night long, so you can rise with the sun and sleep when it's dark.
- Stay asleep. If you stop eating at least two hours before bedtime and stop drinking an hour before bedtime, not only will you sleep better, but also you won't wake up for trips to the bathroom in the middle of the night. What about that glass of hot milk? Well, milk does have tryptophan in it, which increases serotonin and helps you sleep.

5

soothe your hectic life

As a musician who is on the road about 50 weeks of the year, I know what it's like to feel that it's all just too much. My biggest tour dates are during the holiday season, when I bounce around the entire country in some of the worst weather months of the year. In each city, I have sold-out theaters where fans often bring their entire family for a relaxing night of holiday cheer. Believe me when I tell you that this gets stressful when Mother Nature doesn't cooperate. I can't tell you how many times I've sat in an airport and heard this heart-dropping announcement: "Ladies and gentlemen, we're sorry, but there's going to be a delay." I'll go up to the counter, mustering all the calmness in my soul, and ask, "Do you think this flight might actually be canceled?"

"Mr. Brickman, look outside," the nice lady will tell me.

Yes, there is Mother Nature dumping buckets of snow on the tarmac.

What can I do? It's not like I can get to Des Moines a day earlier, because I had a Chicago concert last night. And I know that I can't control Mother Nature, who obviously isn't always a Jim Brickman fan—or maybe she's just a prankster who likes to challenge me during this time of year.

The bottom line here is that in my world I experience stress on a daily basis, and I'm guessing you have your own brand of headache-inducing stress. Maybe it's a report that's due or a project that has hit several snags. Or perhaps it's the fact that *no* seems to be the hardest word, and you have 10 major things to squeeze into one eight-hour work day followed by volunteering at the school bake sale tonight, getting the kids to and from soccer practice, picking up the dry cleaning, going grocery shopping, getting the kids to bed, and then finishing up that big, all-important report for work.

I'm someone who likes to do it all, but how can you do it without driving yourself nuts? Here's what I learned:

become a 15-minute man or woman

There are two kinds of people in life—the ones who get there early and the ones who race in at the last minute, apologizing profusely. Sometimes I think that those people who are

always late want us to believe that they are so darn busy that
we're lucky that they showed up at all. As for me, I'm fortunate that I set my own schedule, and although I could easily
be a late person, I've chosen to become an early bird when it
comes to everything I can control. Of course I can't control a
late flight. I can control that I get to the airport early and
don't have to stress myself out running for the gate. I can't
control a journalist who arrives late for an interview. I can
control that I'm there just a tad early, so I'm not fretting
about keeping someone waiting.

As someone who travels a lot, I've made it my personal
rule to get to the airport 10 to 15 minutes earlier than I need
to be there. If I need to be there an hour early, I'm going to be
there an hour and 15 minutes early. Why? This action dra-
matically lowers my stress levels because I have a little cushion to compensate for Murphy's law: Anything that can go
wrong will go wrong. So what if there's a little extra traffic or
a line at the tollbooth? I'm not freaking out because I have
my cushion. If I didn't have my cushion, the slowness of the
traffic because of construction or the fact that the car needs
gas would turn into a major event. Now it's just a minor blip.
In airports, I have time, so I'll actually walk around, grab a
healthy snack, and even check out new books or go to one of
the shops. I'll return a few calls or write things in my planning book. Those extra 15 minutes are nirvana for a busy person. Think of it as shifting your stress levels from the red
zone back down into neutral.

The 15-minute cushion also works great in the morning.

Mind you, I'm not getting up so much earlier that it changes my day. But those extra 15 minutes in the morning do make a world of difference. I'm not racing around and stressing; I'm actually allowing myself to have a tranquil, slower start to the day that feels so much better.

Can't find my keys? Who cares? I have my 15-minute cushion to realize that for some odd reason I left them on the washing machine. A friend calls to chat for a second? Guess what? I actually have a second. In fact, I have a whole 10 minutes to chat and continue on with my routine.

How great is it to realize you actually *do* have time for that cup of coffee?

The pre-soothed me used to race around the house before leaving in the morning. If it was a flight day, I would tempt fate, push it to the last minute and then hop in a cab to head to the airport. When I'd see the morning traffic, panic would set in. "Do you think we'll make it?" I'd ask the cabbie in a half-crazed voice. When I'd realize that we actually might not make the flight in time, my freak-out gene would kick into higher gear. Suddenly it was the most tension-filled hour ever as we crawled to the airport. Even worse were those mornings when I was running a bit late and then couldn't find a cab for 10 minutes. My freak-out was now in full bloom.

Again, the 15-minute cushion means enough time for a minor glitch and an easy, peaceful ride, knowing that I'll probably arrive at the airport a little bit early. There's power in knowing that time is on your side.

soothe now

If you can't face getting up at 5:45 a.m. instead of 6:00 a.m. try going to bed 15 minutes earlier. With DVRs, there is no need to watch your show in real time. Just wind down and get a little extra sleep so you won't feel so awful when the alarm sounds earlier. What's the real difference between lights out at 10:15 and lights out at 10:30? You might just miss several stressful end-of-the-day news stories saying the world is coming to an end. Why not end your day early and get some extra z's?

let it go

According to a recent Stress in America survey conducted by the American Psychological Association, about half of the population reports being regularly stressed out because they are "unable to control the important things in their life very or fairly often."

If control is key when it comes to de-stressing, then it's crucial to think of ways to get your life under some sort of control.

A few simple tips:

Realize that you really have no control over the future. Of course you can control your future to some extent by taking a new job or moving to another city. In the end, each day offers its surprises; you simply have to embrace the unknown and deal with it.

Know that things happen in their own time. You have to surrender to the natural flow of life, in which everything happens when it's supposed to happen. I spent years struggling as a musician before getting my first record deal. Instead of focusing on the stress of the struggle, I focused on my work, believing that good things would come in the future—and what happened exceeded my wildest expectations.

Treat yourself on stressful days. It's natural to be stressed out about deadlines or the knowledge that you have to deal with a certain high-strung person today. If you have no choice in your daily activities, make sure to take some time for yourself in addition to doing this "chore" you don't really want to do. In between appointments, treat yourself to an extra half hour in the hot tub or take a walk in a beautiful park (great in both winter and summer). Take a moment and look up at the sky. Focus on how the clouds move and take shape. This is a simple exercise that will calm down any frantic mind.

Let go of people who stress you out—if possible—or set boundaries around the ones who do. Let's say you have a particularly high-strung boss who doesn't mind if the entire team works on Thanksgiving or who yells at you to come into her office 20 times during the day. Or maybe there's one coworker who really stresses you out because he's so inept and you're picking up the slack. You can't always choose the people with whom you'll spend your working day, but you can pick the players in your private life. If one of your friends is a constant downer and tries to drown you in her negativity, consider removing her from your life temporarily or forever. You don't want to choose to bring in people who just add to your daily stress. If one of your parents is stressing you out, then you might need to set firm boundaries. Yes, you are drawing a line in the sand here, because some talking is certainly better than not talking. You might have to say to your downer friend, "Mondays are my really hectic day. I'd appreciate it if we could talk later in the week." Or you might have to tell your mother, "I love you, but I'm just not able to talk every morning on the way to work. Let's spend some quality time catching up over the weekend."

Take the case of Michelle, one of my studio singers, whose elderly mother (who lived a mile away) called her every single morning at 6:00 a.m. with a list of complaints. Michelle couldn't even wake up without immediately feeling totally stressed out by a mother who was acting as her alarm clock. Luckily, Michelle's mom's health was good, but she still had a long list of problems ranging from a toilet that wouldn't flush to "I wish I hadn't married your father 50 years ago." Facing a 45-minute commute and a long day at work, Michelle really didn't have time to figure out (before her first cup of coffee) why the plumber hadn't called back yet and if her parents were truly compatible.

Michelle told me that if she didn't answer the phone, her mother would call again and again—until Michelle was forced to answer because she was worried her mother was facing a medical emergency. By the way, Michelle also had to deal with two small children, her own husband, and her busy job. I lovingly told her that she had to take control of this situation with her mother.

Of course, telling Mom that you're not able to talk every single morning may not go over well at first, but there is no choice. We know how stress affects your physical health. A little tough talk with the stress-causing people who can't be phased out of your life isn't pleasant in that moment of truth, but in the long run it can help reduce your stress levels. As for that boss who bellows your name, suggest, "Mary, I can't always hear you when you shout for me. Could you just IM me on the computer and I'll be happy to come into your office?" Think of two or three ways to better manage that stressful situation and be ready to suggest them for your own mental well-being.

simple ways to energize your daily routine

Okay, you really want to get through a day with as little stress as possible, which means you need the energy to face the next 24 hours. Here are some of the best ways to amp up your natural energy to feel better (and thus less stressed) during your daily routine.

Start your day without stimulants. Even though I like my coffee, I have been trying to eliminate it from my day. It takes about 10 days to break your addiction to caffeine in the morning. Try to allow your body to wake up without that artificial jolt. I have to admit that eliminating coffee was awfully hard for me, but at the end of this experiment, I found myself waking up absolutely energized and not even craving the caffeine. Just regaining this natural morning energy, similar to what I felt as a child, reduced my stress

soothe now

The opposite of control is surrendering to circumstances. It's important to realize when you're not in control—a snowstorm, a medical emergency, a child having an accident—and surrender to the fact that life often happens by chance. Your job isn't to be in control every minute, but to deal with the outcome of situations. In other words, surrender and let others drive. Allow someone with far greater skills take the wheel while you work in a support role. I finally had to give in to late plane travel because I don't control nature—that, and I don't know how to fly a plane (yet)!

considerably. No longer was I grumbling about getting my coffee. Instead, I was thinking, *I feel good. A little breakfast and time to hit the gym.*

Get out in the sun. Try to get outside during the breaks in your day. Natural sunlight reduces your stress hormones, lowers your blood pressure, and increases your serotonin levels, which means it's a natural mood lifter. Instead of having cookies at 3:00 in the afternoon and then experiencing a sugar crash, take a quick walk outside to revive yourself.

Hydrate. Most of us don't drink enough water each day and thus walk around dehydrated. This state causes you to feel tired and sluggish, which means you're often stressed out because you can't focus and get the job done. When you feel this way, just drink some water or even splash cool water on your face. The splashing is a way to stimulate circulation and metabolism. Make sure to drink water all day long.

Listen to music throughout the day. This is also a

great way to reduce stress and fatigue, as music increases your natural dopamine levels. A study done at the University of Wisconsin revealed that listening to a familiar singer whose music you like actually boosts your feel-good hormones and decreases stress.

Move your legs. If you have a desk job that requires you to sit for long periods of time, stand up and take frequent walks. You need to move to increase your energy levels. Sitting for too long stresses both your body and your mood. Some offices actually provide an option of a standing desk, which is a great idea. If yours isn't that progressive, then make sure to take a short walk around the place several times a day. Try answering questions sent by e-mail in person. If walking around provokes strange stares, insist that you have a medical need to get the blood flowing. I'm sure your doc would be happy to write you a note saying that sitting for eight hours isn't good for you . . . because it isn't.

Try some aromatherapy. If you have a stressful day ahead or are stuck in an anxiety-ridden career, then practice some aromatherapy in your office or home. Studies show that smelling peppermint, cinnamon, or citrus (oranges and lemons) jump-starts your energy. If you can't have a bowl of oranges at your desk, just buy some essential oils at a natural foods store and dab a little bit of it on your wrist for the same effect.

Have a snack. It's great to know that chewing wakes you up in a way that nothing artificial can. When you chew, you activate your brain, which is a natural way to boost your energy. And if you eat something tart like a grapefruit or even chew sour-flavored gum, it will send your brain a signal that you want a bolt of energy, because a tart taste is a natural stimulant.

how to know if you're overscheduled

There is a fine line between not doing enough and doing too much in any given day. How do you know if you're over-scheduling yourself into a total stress ball? According to research, the clearest indicator is that you're short-tempered. Do you find yourself getting angry with people for no reason? This is a common reaction to the stress of doing too much, which in turn can cause you to get hyper-emotional about everything and nothing.

Here's an example. You race off to a meeting at a restaurant. You sit down and are immediately assaulted by the sound of a baby crying at the next table. You demand that the waiter talk to the baby's parent. Why are you being so high-strung about this situation? Your reaction might not be a response to the baby's crying but to the fact that you're stressed-out in general.

Here are a few other clues that you're turbo-loading your schedule in an unhealthy way:

You're constantly screaming at people. If you're becoming a rageaholic, try the mindful breathing exercises on pages 10–11. Another tip I like is to try to get rid of non-obligatory appointments and replace them with something relaxing. For instance, if you feel you really don't need to be part of your sixth school bake sale of the year, but you would be more than willing to volunteer to accompany your child's class on a school trip spent wandering around a museum, make the change. You'll thank yourself later.

You're always feeling tired and slightly sick. Remember that stress plays upon your health, so constant headaches, stomachaches, and even that nervous, jittery feeling are signs that you're overdoing it with your schedule.

You're always late. Maybe that's your thing—always being late. And your friends even laugh about it: "That Tom, he's never on time. You can count on him being late." The truth is, if you're always late, you're probably trying to do too much. Take out a few variables and you might be on time.

You're a clutter king or queen. Are there piles of stuff cascading all over your kitchen counter or desk? Maybe you don't have a real filing system but are so busy that you just toss everything from bills to catalogs to that college reunion notice on top of the mountain of clutter. If you're too busy to run your own life, it's time to stage an intervention. Hire a clutter expert or spend a long Saturday organizing and throwing out and shredding what you don't need. Set aside a day each week to keep it all organized, or fit in a half hour at work to do the same with your desk.

You can't remember the last time you smiled. If you're just trudging through your day trying to get it all done without much success . . . well, that's no way to live. If you can't remember the last time you smiled or had a bit of fun, then it's time to examine your schedule and weed out what's not necessary. Remember that life is short. You don't always want to spend time doing things out of obligation—such as watching your neighbor's kids for the tenth time.

practice saying no

I'm the master of scheduling about a hundred things into one day. Is that a great way to live? Probably not. I'm often racing from one thing to the other while thinking, *Maybe I should have said no to a few things.* I guess I'm not alone, because most people have a hard time saying no. We will commit to something even when we know that we have little time and cramming in one more thing will really stress us out.

How do you say no? To start with, I've been trying to learn that *no* is a complete sentence. You don't always have to give a reason after that word. Just a simple "No, I'm sorry. I can't do it" will have to suffice. Of course I'd love to help out, honestly I would, but "No, I can't today." Or, as one of my friends who is a personal trainer at my gym likes to say, "I'm not able." He doesn't like to use the word *can't.*

Saying no works like emotional quicksand for a lot of people, especially those who like to please others. But at what cost are you pleasing so many people? You're not saying no enough if you're still doing things that cause you to feel stressed, to lose sleep, or not to do your own work in order to help out in other ways. You're not saying no enough if you feel like you're being used when you say yes. Ask yourself: Are you devoting as much time and energy to yourself as to other people?

Quite often I hear from moms who are juggling kids and a career. One mom told me that she was extremely stressed while spending her free evenings arguing over decorations for a school event with other parents. Most of the time she just sat there and got her opinions shot down, but she participated because she was asked or often bullied into attending. She even continued to take part in the activities when one of the other PTA parents told her that she wasn't color coordinating the streamers in the right fashion. "Jim, I'm not getting to spend time with my kids this week in order to be part of this activity—and a mom is telling me I'm not doing it right. Now I'm really stressed out."

The truth is that most of us say yes because we're afraid of saying no. We think people won't like us or we'll be dubbed a bad person/coworker/parent/son/daughter/human being. You need to know that only you can designate yourself a bad anything. And if you feel that what you're committing to by saying yes will stress you out, then you need to say no. Saying no doesn't mean you're a bad person. You just can't accommodate all people all the time.

Many of us also like to reduce conflict in our lives. We really want to say no, but think it's just easier to say yes. No, you really don't want to drive Sam to the airport because it's a pain to face all that morning traffic, but he will hound you until you say yes. It's true that sometimes this response won't go over well with others, but you have to stick to your guns. You're not saying that you'll *never* drive him to the airport, but next Monday simply isn't going to work for you. Let's say that your neighbor is now a single parent and is constantly looking for babysitters so he can go out. You've done it a couple of times, but now it's becoming a routine. It's necessary to say no to him.

Here are my favorite ways to say no:

○ **I'm sorry, but I'm busy.** Hey, it's usually the truth because most of the time I am busy. This means I can't do something in a certain time. Sometimes I will share with the other person why I'm busy (on tour, in the studio), and other times I will leave an "I'm busy" message and then just move on to the next topic. One note: Don't provide a laundry list of excuses. Just one declarative "I'm busy," followed by a one-sentence detail if you wish.

○ **It's just not a good time.** This is good for those people who pop into town and ask to stay at your house with their seven kids for two weeks. This one doesn't need to be followed up with a reason. It's just not a good time. Can you help with that event? It's just not a good time. Can you drive me downtown? It's just not a good time. Can I borrow $1,000? You get the idea. You don't really have to explain anymore because everyone knows that everyone is super busy these days and time is at a premium.

○ **I'd be happy to help, but . . .** I get asked to play at weddings or parties by a lot friends. Honestly, I would love to help, but I usually have to be somewhere else. This is a nice and easy way of saying

that you don't want this to disrupt your friend-
ship, but it simply won't be possible. I have song-
writers who want to join forces, and sometimes
it's a great idea and other times it isn't. This is how
I say no. You can add, "This is a great idea and I'd
be happy to help, but I'm committed that night."

o **Can I get back to you?** This is for those times
when you really don't know your schedule and you
don't want to be pressured into saying a quick yes
only to figure out you have 10 other things going
on that same night. You're allowed to think about
whether this request fits into your life. It's far better to say that you want to think about it than it is
to tell the person a quick yes and then back out.
Make sure you give some specifics here: "Can I get
back to you? I'll need until Friday, and then I'll
give you an answer."

o **No.** As I said, *no* is a complete sentence. When
asked if you can help this weekend, you can simply
say, "No, I can't." This is to the point and you don't
need to say anything more. A friend of mine had a
pushy next-door neighbor who was always asking
her to pick up items for him at the store, although
there was no real reason he couldn't do it for himself. She did her neighbor favors several times,
getting progressively angrier at him and more
stressed out. In fact, once she saw him racing
around town on his motorcycle while she was
fetching laundry detergent for him. "Jim," she told

me, "I'm being used. He's only 60. In great health. Plays tennis daily. But I'm becoming his errand girl." Finally my friend started singing a chorus of "no's" to this man. Could she go to the store for him? "No. Have a nice day." Could she take those boxes to the post office? "No. Sorry. Bye." He finally got the point—and stopped asking.

Creating a more balanced life makes you feel calm and inspired. Get grounded today with great tips at SootheYourWorld.com.

6

soothe yourself
with meditation

I wish I could say that I was a meditation expert who made sure to escape to a quiet corner each day to clear my mind. Actually I'm new to meditation. Still, I can't deny my curiosity, because each expert quoted in this book has touted the benefits of daily meditation, insisting that you don't have to be some guru sitting on a mountaintop to experience the life-changing effects meditating. I'm game for anything in the name of soothing, so I thought I'd investigate meditation and a few other modalities that are supposed to calm the mind.

why meditate?

I like to arm myself with facts before I start a new program, so I asked the experts, "Why meditate? What will I get out

85

of it?" Here are their answers, culled from a variety of sources:

Meditation reduces pain. According to a study in the *Journal of Neuroscience,* after four 20-minute meditations over four days, a group of adult volunteers rated the same burning pain as 57 percent less unpleasant and 40 percent less intense. Progressive doctors are now sending patients with chronic pain home with instructions on how to meditate. Meditation helps the mind gain control of unpleasant sensations, including pain. Imagine that your mind is a stereo and you're just turning down the pain knob like it's the volume control.

Meditation offers a variety of health boosters. In a study done at Massachusetts General Hospital, patients with high blood pressure tried meditation, and more than half of them enjoyed a significant drop in blood pressure that even reduced how much medication they required. A Mayo Clinic study revealed that meditation is helpful in managing the symptoms of high blood pressure. In addition, it helps your immune system and even eases inflammation. A study done at the University of Wisconsin—Madison found that mindful meditation gave relief to those suffering from chronic inflammatory problems. It has also been known to reduce the risk of heart attacks.

Meditation can make you smarter. In a 2009 UCLA study, MRI scans were given to those who had practiced meditation over their lifetime. Unsurprisingly, various parts of the meditators' brains were much larger than those same parts in a control group that never meditated. One of the regions affected was in the emotional regulation section of the brain. In another study, researchers found that the hippocampal area of the brain and the parts dealing with compassion and self-awareness were enlarged due to meditation. So, if you want more gray matter where it truly does matter, then tuck a little bit of meditation into your daily schedule.

Meditation helps you to relax. Since it's a stress buster, meditation is one of the quickest ways to learn how to relax. Meditation's restorative effects on cognitive function were studied at the University of Michigan. People in the study were given a 35-minute task that left them fatigued. Then they were asked to break up into groups, with one group taking a walk through city streets and the other taking a walk in a large park. Those who did the walk in the park performed much better during an attention test, as they had quieted their minds, unlike those who had walked in the noisy city. In another study, some research subjects looked at 50 pictures of nature and others at pictures of city life. Those who looked at pictures of nature had far greater attention abilities afterward, as opposed to those who looked at the city pictures. People who look at nature and meditate on it replenish themselves far more than those who take in an urban environment.

Meditation can make you a better person. According to a Yale study done in 2013, meditation might just result in higher degrees of compassion. Over an eight-week training session, those who were in a group that meditated had more compassion in situations staged to test compassion than those who did not meditate. In one situation, researchers had a man in crutches (actually an actor) sit in a waiting room pretending to be in pain. Only 15 percent of those who did not meditate offered to help, while 50 percent of those who did meditate helped him. In another study from Emory University, those who meditated on a regular basis showed an increased degree in empathy. That's because meditation activates the part of the brain that recognizes the emotions of other people.

Meditation is helpful to relieve stress. Many studies show that stress, anxiety, and even depression are helped by regular meditation. According to a study done at Johns Hopkins University, mediation may allay anxiety in human beings. Instead of jumping into your usual worry mode, where you escalate a situation from "I'm stuck in traffic, which means I'll miss that call and my boss will be mad and I'll get fired," you learn in meditation how to calm the mind before it falls prey to this stressful anxiety cycle. When you meditate, you learn how to recognize negative thoughts and dismiss them. The deep relaxation of meditation also helps people fall asleep more easily because of reduced stress and anxiety levels. Mindful meditation also leads to a better quality of sleep, according to a 2013 University of Utah study.

how do you meditate?

I love all the healthy aspects of meditation, but I wasn't really sure where to start. I didn't see myself devoting a room at my house to meditation, although I could easily find a corner with no distractions, put down a mat, and make sure there was some soothing music in the background. My major question after I created a meditation spot was simple: *Now what do I do?*

There are some easy ways to get ready to meditate. First, decide that you will devote some time each day to meditation. If you have time, do some simple stretches that allow you to loosen up. And always start by breathing in and out slowly to calm your heart rate and focus your mind. Wear comfortable clothes, turn off your cell phone, and give yourself the gift of relaxation. The great part about meditation is that you can do it anywhere and you don't need to devote hours to see results: Just 10 minutes will do.

One note: When you're new to meditation, your mind will wander. You might even think meditation is sort of silly or hard. Each time you feel that way, just pull your focus back to your breathing. Let all that chatter in your mind fall away; imagine having a broom in your head and sweeping the distractions away.

Many books and instructional CDs will take you through guided meditations, telling you what to do at each step of the way. The most important thing is to carve out undisturbed time. You can even light a candle to set the mood and focus your attention. Don't worry about doing it wrong. You're in the moment and doing the best that you can, which is the point.

Here are a few of my favorite ways to start meditating.

Ocean Meditation: Put on soothing music. Get into a comfortable, quiet spot. Sit tall with your hands palms-up on your lap. Take several really deep breaths, continuing this for one minute or more depending on how stressed out you are. Feel calm wash over you like ocean waves. If you prefer to do this without music, you can just be silent and listen to yourself breathe. Try not to think about anything. If negative thoughts come into your mind, pretend that an ocean wave is sweeping them out to sea for good.

Reboot-Your-Mind Meditation: This is a meditation to do when you're stuck in traffic. Choose a mantra for yourself. You can use "Life is joyful" or "I'm calm and relaxed" or a phrase of your choice. If you're in a stressful situation, tune out and repeat your mantra to yourself out loud or in your head. This might not sound like a meditation, but it is. I have a friend who says, "Life is perfect the way that it is." He says it over and over again when stuck in horrible California traffic. Just saying his mantra calms him down.

Yale Meditation: This one comes from Yale Medical School and is another meditation that you can try anywhere. You can do this sitting or lying down. Sit or lie down, close your eyes, and breathe slowly. Shift from chest breathing to deep abdominal breathing. Count down from 10 to zero. Repeat as many times as necessary. You can listen to soft music or do this in silence, and you can do it at any time, anywhere.

Calming Meditation: Sit or lie down in a comfortable position. Close your eyes and relax until you're breathing slowly from your abdomen. Think the word *calm* as you calm your mind down. At the same time, imagine that a different body part is melting into relaxation with each breath that you take. Do this systematically by starting at the top of your head, inhaling and exhaling as you relax each body part and think the word *calm*. Work your way down your body—face, neck, chest, etc. Pick different body parts including your temples or the back of your knees. Feel each part melt into total relaxation as you calm it with your mind.

Five Clouds Meditation: This comes from traditional Chinese medicine and is called Five Clouds Meditation because it's believed that there are five organ systems in the body and five elements. Give each of the five organs that are traditionally part of this meditation a color: green for the liver, red for the heart, yellow for the spleen, white for the lungs, and blue for the kidneys. Sit in a relaxed pose, breathe, calm yourself, and then imagine a cloud of color completely surrounding that organ. Take several minutes for each organ. When you've visualized each of the five color clouds, then see all the colors bursting into a rainbow.

Headache-Buster Meditation: Are you prone to headaches? Check out this meditation, which is a surefire headache buster. In a dark room or one with the lights dimmed, sit quietly with your eyes closed. Breathe in through your nose and let air fill your abdomen as if you're filling a balloon. Hold that breath inside your abdomen for five seconds. Exhale slowly through your mouth. This meditation is also good to help lower your blood pressure.

massage therapy

Massage is a great way to get rid of your weekly stress. I love every part of the process of getting a massage, including sitting in a cushy chair at a spa before they call you in for even more relaxation with a qualified therapist who works the knots out of your back and neck. I thought it was amazing that studies show that massage doesn't really change your psychological makeup, but since most people think that it calms them, the effects are actually the same and therefore anxieties disappear.

Even a simple five-minute massage helps to reduce anxiety, so learn a few techniques online and try them with your partner. If you're having a facial or a mani-pedi, always say yes to the complimentary foot or hand massage because of the above effect.

decompress with yoga

I've only dabbled in yoga, so I'm not an expert, but I do know that it feels good when you let the stress of the day evaporate while you concentrate on doing a simple downward-facing dog. On a stressful day, I like to do five simple poses that help to calm me down and stretch my body.

mountain pose

Stand tall with your feet together and relax your shoulders. At the same time, shift your weight so it's evenly distributed on the soles of your feet.

Place your arms at your side.

Variation: Breathe deeply and raise your arms over your head, with your palms facing each other. Reach up as if you're trying to touch the sky with your fingertips.

warrior 2

Stand with your legs three to four feet apart. Turn your left foot 90 degrees to the left, and your right foot just slightly to the left.

Gently lift your hands to your hips and relax your shoulders. Slowly extend your arms straight out to the sides with your palms facing down, fingers open.

Look toward your left fingers and inhale. As you exhale, bend your left leg until your knee is over your left ankle, at about 90 degrees. Hold this pose for 30 seconds, then straighten your left knee, lower your arms and switch sides. Remember to breathe deeply throughout your practice.

tree pose

Stand tall with your arms at your side.

Place your body weight on your left leg and then take the sole of your right foot inside your left thigh; don't rest your right foot directly on the inside of your left knee—place it above, on the inner thigh, or below, on the inner calf. Make sure your hips face forward.

When you find balance, move your hands in front of you in a prayer pose, palms together at your heart.

Inhale and extend your arms into the air and separate your palms while they face each other. Stay in this pose for 30 seconds.

Lower your arms and repeat with your right foot on the ground and your left foot on your inner right thigh (or calf).

eagle pose

Start in Mountain Pose with your arms at your sides, your back straight and your shoulders relaxed.

Bend slightly at the knees and lift your right leg. Move your right leg so that your knee is resting on your left thigh. Now wrap your right foot around the back of your left calf. If you have trouble balancing, you can place your right foot on the ground to the left of your left foot.

Keeping your legs wrapped, bring both arms in front of you with your elbows bent and your fingers pointing toward the ceiling. Next, move your left elbow on top of your right elbow so that you can touch the backs of your hands together. You can take your hand pose further by moving your right hand toward your face, and continuing to wrap your right hand around your left wrist so that your palms touch.

Hold this pose for 20 to 30 seconds, remembering to breathe. If you have trouble balancing, just keep practicing! Everything seems impossible until it becomes possible.

cobra

Lie on the floor facedown, hands directly beneath your shoulders and legs extended, with the tops of your feet resting on the floor.

Tuck your hips down and squeeze your glutes.

Press your shoulder blades down your back and push through your thumbs and index finger as you lift your chest up as far as you can go without hurting your back.

soothe expert:

Kristin McGee on Yoga

Celebrity yoga and Pilate's instructor and *Health* magazine contribut-
ing editor Kristin McGee knows that yoga is one of the best ways to
relax. "We hold our issues in our tissues," she says.

DON'T FRET IF YOU CAN'T GET TO A CLASS

You can do yoga anywhere! All you need is your own body. You can
use a mat—or not! A towel or a carpeted floor works fine. Find a quiet
corner in your home and dedicate it as your personal yoga retreat.

YOGA DOESN'T HAVE TO TAKE AN HOUR

You can do yoga for just 5-15 minutes a day and still get stress-relieving
benefits. If you're super-stressed right now, try Standing Forward Hang
(see below): Let the blood flow to your head and allow the weight to
release from your shoulders. It will instantly change your mood.

YOGA IS NOT COMPETITIVE

What if you're not as bendy as the woman next to you? Don't get frus-
trated. Yoga is a process of learning about your body and discovering
what your body can do for you. There are 300 different yoga poses to
choose from and you can and will find the ones you enjoy. Trying new
poses is part of the fun.

ONE POSE ANYONE CAN (AND SHOULD) TRY

Standing Forward Hang. Stand with your feet hip width apart and hinge
forward from your hips, bending forward and letting your arms hang overhead. Bend your knees if you need to and don't lock your knees. Engage
your abdominals and let your shoulders head and neck relax. Inhale and
exhale for 5 to 8 counts, before slowly rounding up to stand.

more meditative practices

The list is endless, but here are a few other ways you can turn up your stress-busting techniques.

- Crank up your tunes. It doesn't matter if you're listening to hard rock, jazz, the Rolling Stones, or my music. Research from the University of Maryland shows that music relaxes your blood vessels and increases blood flow. This is a great way to calm down and support heart health.

- Give into temptation to have a good cry. A good cry actually does make you feel better, say biochemical researchers, who found that 85 percent of women like to cry it out in order to feel better . . . and do so on a regular basis.

- Get moving. A boost of hard exercise works wonders. Try racing your kids down the street or chasing after your dog in the yard as an instantaneous way to lower your stress levels.

- Try a quick acupuncture-acupressure technique. For an instant bout of stress relief, apply firm pressure on the skin between your index finger and thumb, which in Chinese medicine is an acupressure point called the hoku spot. In about 30 seconds, this technique releases tension by 39 percent, according to a study done at Hong Kong Polytechnic University.

7

soothe your need to do everything

While I was in Nashville recently, I ran into a musician friend.

"Oh, hey, how are you doing?" I asked him. "What are you doing? What's going on?"

He smiled and said, "I'm great. As for what's going on? I got a whole lot of nothing going on these days." His grin was genuine, and at that moment I realized he wasn't depressed about having nothing going on, but was actually blissful about it.

When do you ever hear someone say aloud to anybody that they're happy doing nothing? Usually when you run into someone, it's a bit of a competition to say either what you're doing or what your family is up to these days. You disgorge this list of activities that makes you sound like you're living a full, extremely hectic life, which should thus be celebrated.

Isn't it okay to celebrate someone who is taking a little breather? That day my old musician friend didn't dazzle me with the names of the musicians he was working with or the exotic places he would visit on tour or on vacation. He said he was happy to be spending the season at home just hanging out and working on his house. I knew my friend had plenty of money to take a little time off, and he had worked very hard in the past. Yet I felt like something was wrong. Shouldn't he (I was really thinking about myself) be doing something great all of the time? Didn't taking some "nothing time" mean that you weren't hot anymore or that no one was calling? Wasn't that a fast track to failure?

When I really thought about this, I decided that I should revise my thinking. Hadn't I earned the right through all my hard work to take a little time off to do nothing and recharge my batteries? Could I also admit to someone that I wasn't doing anything for the next few weeks? Granted, that would be hard for me because I'm always thinking about the next CD and the next project. The question remained: Why wasn't the idea of taking a little time off actually a good thing?

Maybe we can trace this uneasy feeling when it comes to rest and relaxation back to childhood, when we were taught that there was real shame in washhting time. I remember the old saying "Idle hands are the devil's tools." We were taught that we had to always be productive, or at least I was schooled in that theory. When I told my mother I had nothing to do and was bored, she always had the same response: "You have nothing to do? I'll find you something to do." That something usually involved Windex, so I learned to stop complaining and figured out what to do by myself.

Of course, you don't want to strive to do nothing all the time. We all have those friends who spend most of the day in a robe and . . . well, that's not my way to live. Yet occasionally it would be nice to have nothing on the slate. It would be great to shower, get dressed, eat a little breakfast, and then go outside to see where the day might take me. Would I go left or right when I hit the sidewalk? Would I go downtown or hit the country? It reminds me of the lyrics in that great song performed by Bruno Mars about taking a day to do "nothing at all." I think the younger generation, dubbed the millennials, are much better at having a nothing day than we boomers are. Somewhere there must be a good balance.

soothe now

Try it. Take a whole Friday or Saturday off from life. Tell everyone that you're unavailable and plan for it to be that way. Have your mate get the kids to a playdate and declare that it's a "me day." Don't fill up your day with chores either. This is about just experiencing life and doing what you consider fun. Go to the woods for a walk or go see a mindless double feature. Check out a play or go to that spa and maybe catch a musician at a bar. Make sure that you don't have too many plans. Allow the natural flow of the day to guide you.

practice the art of silence on your me day

Shhhhhh . . . can you hear the silence? If your world is filled with sound, I'm advising you to go somewhere extremely quiet and just listen to nothing for a whole 5 minutes. This might drive some people crazy, but it can also be a great way to relax. I don't mean you have to tune out all sounds, but try to find a spot where you can eliminate as many sounds as possible. A public park with dogs barking isn't a good option, but your house while everyone is at the movies is a great one. Turn off the TV and music. Just sit in silence on the couch or in your favorite chair. Allow your mind to wander and see where it goes. In those moments of absolute quiet, I find myself thinking of new music. Maybe that moment will fuel your creativity, too. The important part of this exercise is to just allow yourself to be in the moment. If 5 minutes isn't enough for you, then try to do 10 minutes or 20—whatever works for you.

This exercise can lower your blood pressure and make your stress levels really plummet. Use it again and again during highly stressful periods of your life. It's as if you've got the remote in your hand and you're selecting a channel that's just about you and your thoughts. Allow yourself to unwind and let go of any mental anxiety you might have been experiencing. During this time try to sweep away anything that causes you stress and focus on the positive aspects of your life. You'll be surprised at what you will resolve in total silence.

a monastery where you live in silence

I found out about the joys of silence in an odd way. I hap-pened to be in Nashville meeting with executives of a coun-try record label. I walked into this gorgeous suite of offices and was greeted by a lovely woman named Cindy. "Hi, I'm Jim Brickman." She replied, "I know who you are. I have all of your albums."

"Thank you so much. I'm always surprised when some-one knows me," I said to her. Cindy went on to tell me that she loved my music. "It's just so soothing," she said. Then she said something else that stuck with me.

"You know, the world is just so crazy," she said. "There is just so much noise everywhere." We started to talk and she told me that my music wasn't the only thing she turned to for a little relaxation. "Have you ever heard of this monastery in Kentucky? It's one of the oldest monasteries around. I just went there to live in silence."

She was talking about the Abbey of Our Lady of Gethse-mani near Bardstown, Kentucky. This is a place where Trap-pist monks have lived, prayed, and worked for over 150 years. I decided to check into their prayer and recollection retreat, which they state is a "monastic milieu that offers a place apart to entertain silence in the heart and listen to the voice of God—and to pray for your own discovery." I found out that these monks believe that communicating with God requires solitude and stillness and that "silence fosters and preserves the climate of prayer." It turns out that during this retreat, speaking is permitted only in designated areas. During the day, you can walk acres of woodlands that afford space for reflection. Each guest has a private room with his or her own bathroom and there are modern comforts like air conditioning, but there are no TVs or electronic devices. A library is available, and there are group prayer sessions, but you aren't obligated to participate, as your retreat is unstructured and undirected. You can also have private, silent time with one of the monks.

Cindy chose to participate in their silence retreat, in which you don't talk for three days. Days are spent doing activities such as taking long walks in the woods. Your sole mission is to be in silence with yourself.

"How did you feel when you left the place?" I asked her.

"Completely rejuvenated, Jim," she said. "I also felt closer to God and to myself." Here was a woman who got more rest and rejuvenation out of three days of silence than I got out of two expensive weeks in Maui, during which I was on my cell phone half the time tending to business affairs.

At first I thought it might actually be impossible for me to go three whole days without talking. What if I needed to call someone? What if I read an e-mail and needed to talk out an issue? What if I knew my parents needed me? But after giving Cindy's experience more thought, I decided to dabble in designated periods of silence, periods when I devote my time to nothing and no one but myself (though I still don't think I can ever manage to go three whole days!). I encourage you to try it as well. It can be incredibly liberating to be alone with your thoughts.

soothe now

Did you know that while the average child laughs 140 times a day, an adult laughs only 12 to 14 times a day? Doctors say that you need to find ways to laugh because each time you do, endorphins are released. Studies show that endorphins are 18 to 33 times stronger than morphine when it comes to making you feel better.

I tried the new "laughter yoga," a practice that reminds us of the childish playfulness in every adult. This form of yoga involves laughter as a form of exercise. The laughter might sound forced at first, but believe me when I tell you that it leads to genuine laughter. It also helps to get you out of your own head, thereby reducing your stress and working against your negative thought patterns. (By the way, even faking laughter still releases those stress-killing feel-good endorphins.) Laughter yoga is just a way of saying that you need to exercise your laughing self. Find out what tickles you, maybe literally, and give into it. Often it's healthy and soothing.

By the way, laughter in general oxygenates your body and brain because it causes you to breathe deeply. The result is that you naturally feel healthier and more energetic.

find soothing ways to pass the time

Let's say you've convinced yourself to have a nothing day or week. Or.... month! You might start wondering, "What can I do with my time?" There are many great ways to fill your hours that will make you feel good. But psychologists offer other ways to soothe yourself if you have a few minutes. Now that you have more than just a few, maybe you should try something new.

Let your jaw relax. Most of us can measure our tension by what's going on in our jaw. Here's a quick exercise to reduce the stress: Open your mouth wide for 30 seconds and breathe naturally through your nose. Feel the stretching motion. After the 30 seconds, allow your mouth to gently and slowly close.

Write it all down. There is something to be said about keeping a journal. Now that you have a few minutes to actually think, try writing down your thoughts. Plan to do this on a daily basis, even if you only have 10 to 15 minutes, although you could do this for a much longer period of time. It is a wonderful way to explore your life and figure out what's working and what's not. You'll also find reviewing your journal at the end of the year a great way to explore your accomplishments and figure out what you want to do over again.

Make a list . . . and check it often. Most of us make a grocery list. Why not make a list of what you feel good about in your life and add to it every day? When we're stressed, it's easy to lose sight of what's positive in our lives and focus only on the negative. When you write down all the positives, you suddenly have written proof that life might not be as dramatic or as stressful as you think. You can even do this on sticky notes and place the notes in areas where you tend to feel stress (like in your bathroom, where you get ready in the morning, or in your car). It's time to focus on the positive.

8

soothe
your family
relationships

I guess this is the chapter where I'm supposed to tell you the horrors of being a baby boomer with parents who bug me all the time. Friends share hilarious tales about elderly parents who call them at four in the morning to talk about how their cable just went out and the mean lady on the other end of the phone line was rude and didn't understand their need for HBO, or about a family issue that happened back in the sixties. Maybe it's not the cool thing to say, but my parents are pretty great. I really love them and try to be with them as much as possible.

My parents divorced when I was 12. After years apart living very full lives, however, my folks realized that they still loved each other, were pretty compatible, and could have fun together while being there for each other. So about 8 years ago, they reunited and moved back in together! Frankly, I was thrilled because I'm on the road, and it made me so happy that neither of them was alone.

Peaceful family relationships certainly aren't the norm, and many of my friends and coworkers attribute the bulk of their angst to dealing with extended family members. Of course coping with the health issues of members of your family is extremely stressful, but everything else should fall lower on the stress meter. I believe stress and family issues come down to how much you allow everything to bother you. If you choose to ignore the bad stuff when you're with family, you might just get in that quality time that you crave.

For instance, I was planning to have my dad on my radio show for Father's Day, so I said, "I'll call you Monday at two in the afternoon." He said, "Let me check my book. I'm not available at two. Can we do it Wednesday at four?" I thought that being on the radio would be exciting for him and that he would drop everything, but I didn't realize that he already had a complex schedule of activities. His exercise class on Mondays keeps him happy and healthy. The bottom line was that I would have to work around his schedule, so I decided to accept that and move on rather than dwell on a minor inconvenience.

Even though both of my parents are retired, they're out more evenings than I am. If I said, "Mom, would you like to come with me to the Grammys?" I'd probably hear, "But that's the night we go to yoga followed by salsa dancing! Can they change the date?"

soothe now

With family relations, try to laugh about conflicts and let them go instead of dwelling on them and letting resentments eat you alive. The stress isn't good for anyone involved. Yes, it's annoying that when you go out to eat with your mom, she insists you drop her off in front of the restaurant just in case of rain (even if it's 100 percent sunny outside). Sometimes you just have to shake off your annoyance and agree to do things that really aren't harming you. If you get into a battle of wills about every small detail, there are bound to be hurt feelings, which may linger and turn into lasting hostilities.

dealing with family stresses

Laughing about stress in the family helps, although I know so many friends who treat family relationships like their own mini *Game of Thrones*. Luckily, nobody in their families gets beheaded like on the HBO series, but thanks to unresolved issues, there are still tense moments. Either you can laugh about how your family operates or you can pick apart every single word and action while drawing the battle lines. As you try to negotiate family holidays and outings, it can feel as though your family is at war. In one case I know, just choosing which side of the family will get the coveted Thanksgiving and Christmas visits requires UN-like negotiations, with, as they say, tensions remaining on both sides.

letting go of grudges

Sometimes I lament that I don't get to spend enough alone time with my parents. I have a brother I love and a large extended family, which means when the Brickmans get together, we all have a great time. I find that if I can visit with my parents one-on-one, the conversation can get really interesting. But when there are grandchildren around, there is little time for those heart-to-heart talks. Plus, when you have a group, it's almost inevitable that someone's buttons will get pushed.

This brings me to my mother, the wise Sally Brickman.

When I was in my early teens, my father left my mother for another woman. If and when this woman's name comes up for any reason, it really does push my mom's buttons. But after my mother remarried, then divorced that man and reunited with my father about 8 years ago, she passed on an important soothing lesson to me.

"Yes, things happened in the past," she told me. "I could hang on to those things and be really angry. But if I don't let those negative feelings go away, I can't enjoy your father now. And where we are in our relationship now is really different from then.

"If I hang on to what he did when he was 35, I wouldn't have become a single mother who moved to Chicago and had this interesting other chapter of my life," she told me. "I became more independent because of that experience. I wouldn't have had all the experiences I enjoyed in Chicago if your father hadn't have left. I found *me*."

I really have to applaud my mother here for her wisdom

and her ability to calm a situation. Other people would certainly have said in anger, "I can't believe you did this to me! I will never forgive you!" But my mom knows that because her life unfolded the way it did, she got a chance to find herself and have other joyful experiences. She also learned how to forgive, in contrast to others who never forgive and never forget. The result is that she has a beautiful new relationship with my father, and our family has healed as we live in the moment without dwelling on past hurt. That fact that I can get together with both my mother and my father for vacations and family outings is wonderful.

the parent trap

Some find their relationship as adults with their parents and siblings (and beyond) filled with strife. As a baby boomer, you may know that feeling of guilt when you can't be there for your parent even if "there" is a quick trip to Bed Bath & Beyond for a new shower curtain. Honestly, you feel like a bad person when you say no.

I'm lucky in that my parents aren't "guilters," although I know so many boomers whose parents can really lay on the guilt in a major way. Many times, these parents will bring out the age-old story that begins with "I took you to all those soccer games and school events in 10 feet of deep snow across mountain ranges, and now all I'm asking you for is a ride to the mall." It's stressful and exhausting. (Never fear: I have an amazing expert that will help us in a moment!) Or perhaps

(continued on page 112)

and now a moment with sally brickman, my mom

Q **Tell us about being the single mother of two boys.**

A We were like the Three Musketeers. We really were, and still are, there for each other. It wasn't always perfect, because I raised two active boys. Someone would slam the car door on someone else. You would fight. But the bottom line is that we were always a strong unit.

Q **Tell us about the stresses of being a single parent.**

A Being a single parent, you can't turn to someone and say, "What do you think we should do about this situation? Michael is lighting matches behind the garage!" My style of dealing with it wasn't grounding your kids. Half the time, right or wrong, I put the "guilts" on you. I must have made them feel bad about it!

Q **What is your best advice for mom stress?**

A The bottom line is, I made my sons feel responsible for themselves. I didn't hover over you and solve all your problems and do all your homework. You had jobs. When you said to me, "Gosh, everybody at school has a car." I said, "That's fine, you can get a lot of rides if everybody has a car." You knew if you wanted extra cash, you got a job. And you both had jobs all the time. You respected the fact that I was working—it wasn't a bad thing. You boys handled the household. I think parents should make kids responsible.

Q **And you were always there for us.**

A It's crucial for children not to stress out but to trust their parent or parents. If I said I'd be there at a certain time, I was there. It's so important for kids to feel safe in knowing that you will keep your word.

Q **You've gotten back together with Dad after all these years. How was it to come back to each other?**

A There is a lot of past emotion involved, but more than anything, it's a question of enjoying each other's company. We have a lot of history and want to spend these years together. In fact, one of the things we're doing this summer is going to our 60th high school reunion. We are the only people from a 300-person class who are still together!

Q **Why get back together?**

A We've always enjoyed each other. There is love there. We have two sons together! There are times when it's a little hard to get over what happened when he started another family, but we really get along very well. You just have to block out some of those more difficult times. They do pop up once in a while because we're human. I try to think positively and enjoy the moment. There are so many good things in my life. And there were so many good things from our parting all those years ago when we divorced. I made a wonderful life for myself. I've had a lot of good friends and success in my work.

(continued)

Q So, as you say, Mom, don't live in the past.

A We're living in the now.

Q What do you think about when you want to soothe?

A From the time you were 21 years old, you were taking Michael and me on family vacations. We went to Florida and a number of places. It was just the three of us. We have great memories of those times, and they're amazing to remember now when I want to soothe.

Q Okay, Mom, you can tell one story about me. Please don't stress me out too much!

A Well, James, you were always the dependable one who just wanted to play piano. I do have a funny story and I still have the piece of paper from it. You left a note for the tooth fairy that said: "Dear Tooth Fairy, I have lost the tooth, so I can't put it under my pillow. Would you please give me credit for

you've had a really crazy week at work or with your own family and your father calls and says (in that slightly disappointed tone), "I guess you're too busy to call your ol' dad. You just don't care about me anymore." All of a sudden, your stress meter hits the red. You're wondering, "Am I a bad daughter/son? Am I a bad person?" Then reality sets in and you remind your stressed-out self that you just called him yesterday and talked for two hours.

that and leave the money?" This was when you were three or four. You was wheeling and dealing with the tooth fairy!

Q You've said it's nice to be there for each other

A Yes. The things that come up—doctor visits, holiday times, taking care of and supporting each other—are really special things in our lives right now. We have compassion for and support each other, and the companionship is wonderful at this stage of our lives.

Q Any last advice to combat parental stress?

A Let go just a little bit and give your children some independence and responsibility. I have a grandson and I even tell his father, "You also don't have to spend every moment with your kids." I think giving the children a little more freedom allows the parents time to de-stress. And take a little time for yourself as a parent. The child will survive and probably survive a lot better if Mom and Dad are happier.

sibling issues as adults

When you have a sibling, people might ask you, "Doesn't your sister or brother drive you nuts?" In my case, I have one brother, and we're as different as night and day. I'd think that one of us is adopted and not from our parents, but that's not the case. We're polar opposites in that he's a sunny, happy-go-lucky guy all of the time and I'm more the brooding, introspective musician. He laughs about his struggles in life, whereas I'm constantly worried. His mantra is: It will all be fine. My mantra is: It probably will be fine ... unless everything collapses around us, in which case it won't be fine at all—not that this will probably happen, but I'll go ahead and worry about it, thank you very much.

My brother was very popular when we were kids in school, and I don't mind admitting that it was hard for me to accept. He was really good at sports (and everything else), and everyone liked him. He was also accident-prone, slamming the car door on his arm and then breaking his leg, which meant he got even more attention. I didn't break anything, darn the luck!

He even had great taste in music—and music was supposed to be *my* thing! I couldn't fault him for being into Boston and Steely Dan, although he drove me out of my mind playing Steely Dan's *Asia* album. When we were kids, I would yell, "Turn that off! If I hear 'Deacon Blues' one more time, I'll scream." My brother would just laugh and turn it up while his friends would say, "We love that album."

In our younger days, we did the requisite amount of fighting. But then our mom got remarried when I was in junior high school, and her new husband and his two kids moved in with us. This forced my brother and me to share a room with bunk beds. Suddenly, we stopped whaling on each other and became a solid team against these "intruders" into our lives. It was us against them.

We became close as adults and stayed in touch as much as possible, but then something happened that drew us even closer. One cold February day, while he was working for a

bank in Cincinnati, bank robbers slashed the tires on his car. They waited in the parking lot for him to go out to lunch, and when he noticed his tire was slashed and bent down to check it out, they jumped him. One guy held a gun on him and another stabbed him as they demanded the keys to the bank and its vault so they could go in and rob it.

"I wouldn't have given them the keys," my brother Michael says. "But these were really bad guys and killers."

My brother was due to get married in two weeks, and his stabbing set off a horrifying chain of events during what should have been a happy family time. When he was rushed to the hospital, his condition was critical and the doctors weren't sure if he would survive. Luckily, the knife missed his lung by a fraction of an inch, but his lung still collapsed. "It could have been a lot worse," says Michael. "I was really fortunate because I could have easily gone the way of another victim in a robbery from these guys. She died instantly."

A crisis like this, though clearly unwanted, bonds a family. At the time of his stabbing, I was young and trying to break into the music business. I received a call from my mother, who said through her tears, "Something horrible has happened to your brother." I was in shock because the idea of losing my brother was unfathomable.

It was touch and go for a while; my father, mother, and I hovered around his hospital bed with his fiancée. It about killed me to see happy-go-lucky, laughing Michael fighting for his life. The unfairness of it all left a bitter taste in my mouth. We should have been preparing for their wedding, not hearing words like "We're not sure if he will pull through. He has lost a lot of blood."

(continued on page 120)

soothe expert:

Peggy Wagner
on Family Relationships

Peggy Wagner, LPC, CTRS, is a licensed professor counselor at Sierra Tucson in Tucson, Arizona. She owns and operates Out West Wilderness, LLC, in Tucson and Almont, Colorado, and for 11 years was a counselor at the Canyon Ranch Resort in Arizona. She is also the coauthor of *The Everest Principle: How to Achieve the Summit of Your Life*. Here is her advice for dealing with family stress and strain.

RECOGNIZE FAMILY STRESS

The next time you're around family, increase your awareness and listen to your body. Is your heart rate elevated? Do you feel tense? Do you feel sick to your stomach after a conversation? There is good stress and bad stress. Yes, family interaction can be stressful, but is it so stressful to you that you're having trouble breathing and your heart is racing? Do you feel exhausted or depressed after encounters or conflicts? You have the power and right to pause and ask for some time before making important decisions. When we make decisions in the height of emotion, we often don't make the healthiest ones. Take a moment to breathe, consider both sides of the story, add in the facts, and then make a choice of what to do next.

RELIEVE STRESS IN THE MOMENT

If I'm feeling a little tension, I like to breathe in for a count of four or five and out for a count of five or six. Push the air out for longer than you

breathe in. That's the formula for a relaxation breath. It's also the fastest way to get grounded. Another great tactic is to stop focusing on what is stressing you out, like an argument with your mother, and focus on your senses. What do you smell in that moment? Focus on that lemony smell or the freshly cut grass outside. Focus on what you're seeing or hearing. I'm a tactile person, so if I'm stressed out, I will grab the bottom of my sweater and really focus on how it feels. I'm instantly grounded because I, like everyone else, can usually only think of one thing at a time. Notice textures, sounds, tastes, sights, and smells. When you give yourself a few moments of escape or feeling grounded, you can return to the situation and it will seem more manageable.

RELEASE FAMILIAL GUILT

Older parents can be a stressful situation because we worry so much about them. As adult children, we have to realize that there are things we do have control over and things that we do not have control over, such as chronic illness and aging behaviors. When we stay focused on these issues, we often do not pay attention to our own self-care. Some grown children feel too guilty to have any fun in their lives because they're dealing with older parents. That's not fair. You do need to have breaks from these situations, times when you go out and enjoy yourself. Take the time to engage in your passions. You can spend the time alone or with friends. The point is, you must develop your own happiness. Then you can come back and handle the situation, which may include taking care of an older parent. When you take time out, you will handle things in a way that is more beneficial to both their health and yours. You need some relaxation in your life.

SET LIMITS

Sometimes parents or other relatives consume a lot of your time. They are the first to call in the morning, are apt to call repeatedly during the day, and can potentially pile on requests. Learn to set boundaries. Remember that we have several identities in life—professional, sister, mother, daughter, son, friend, or volunteer. You shouldn't spend all your time or energy in just one of those identities. When an aging parent consumes too much time and energy, you need to set limits. If you don't, you might look for external factors for self-fulfillment—alcohol, cigarettes, food—or you might spend all your money shopping or gambling. If we're not happy inside, we look for external factors. If you keep your life and roles in balance, you won't be as stressed and look for external factors for internal fulfillment. The reality is, you need to look internally and figure out what you need. If you need more time, you must tell your aging parent that you also have needs. You must have the talk.

FOCUS ON THE POSITIVE

At your next family gathering, choose to engage in healthy conversations—those that are forward moving. Yes, you might need to see a family member you dread talking to, or someone might bring up a sore subject. Don't change the subject to avoid it. Simply say, "I'll talk to you about things that are healthy. Or I'm willing to discuss this if we talk in a healthy way. Let's not rehash that." Remember that you can step out of a conversation at any time. If you stand there and fight the same fight, then you're giving your power away.

Remember to keep a healthy energy around you. You decided how much energy you give everyone. If someone is toxic and dragging you down, address it and move on. You can say, "When we have this conversation, we just ruminate. I'm going to choose not to have it." That's much better than awkwardly changing the subject and saying, "Hey, did you see this movie?" You can try to distract them with a subject change, but the bottom line is that if they're draining your energy, then refocus or walk away. People do only what gets reinforced, and if we continue to engage, we are sending that message that what is going on is okay. There are enough healthy people to share your energy with in life.

Another healthy conversation tip is to use the "sandwich" method when addressing something: compliment for the top bun, the meat (or tofu) of the matter in the middle to mention what needs to be addressed, and a compliment for the bottom bun. For example: "I love you so much. But when you smoke, drink, or don't exercise, I worry about your health. Yet I don't want to be a nag. I want you to be around as long as possible to spend as much time with you as I can because I love you so much." This prevents the recipient from getting defensive while still surrounding them with the truth. Remember: Don't give your power away. Try to stay away from giving someone your time or energy if the person is going to fight with you. Remember that you write the script. Just be mindful and aware of your strong reactions and get yourself back to that neutral place.

Thankfully, Michael not only pulled through but actually got married on the originally scheduled date. He's been happily married for 25 years and is a father. These days he lives just outside New York City and is a very talented and creative marketing director. What happened to him brought us even closer. Michael even worked for me for five years running my Brickhouse online marketing company, and we meshed very well together in that arena, too.

Recently I asked Michael how he copes with stress, given what had happened to him:

"Each day when I wake up, I appreciate life. This happened when I was 24 years old and felt like I had my whole life in front of me. Getting stabbed and nearly losing my life really made me appreciate life in general and take a more relaxed attitude toward life," says Michael. "Something like that happens, it puts everything in perspective. Something stressful happens now and I know, 'It's not that bad.' A stressful day at work—not that bad. Traffic—who cares? I enjoy the days, and live in the present.

"It was a normal Tuesday in February when this happened to me," he says. "Now my motto is 'One day at a time— and enjoy that day.'"

By the way, the men who hurt my brother are currently on death row.

I can't even put into words what almost losing my brother did to me. We're so glad to spend time with each other now. It does soothe me to know that if something ever happened to me—anywhere on this earth—my brother would be on the next plane to my side.

9

soothe by moving it

I'm someone who is in perpetual motion. Even when I talk on the phone, I have to move around. Because of all this activity, you'd think I would weigh three ounces by this point, but that's not exactly the case. Instead, I'm still that guy who has to get on the treadmill and show up for training sessions several times a week. If I'm in Minneapolis, I'm hiking the lakes. In Cleveland, I'm at the gym. If I'm in New York, I'm working out with a trainer who pushes me so hard that I'm always amazed that I don't actually pass out.

am i a "before" or an "after"?

So, before we get to all the reasons that exercise is great for stress relief, I want to address a big question that was

soothe now

You have permission to understand and indulge a bit in what soothes you if it doesn't hurt you. A glass of wine is okay; a fifth of vodka is another thing (and seek help if you're using alcohol to solve problems). Have a little chocolate, but not the whole cake.

stressing me out: am I a "before" or an "after"? Here's how the question came up. In general, I'm in pretty good shape (although I have this persistent little gut lately that most of us gain at a certain age; I have perfected the fine art of sucking it in), but I could easily pick myself apart with criticism. A trainer once told me, "I could get you some definition in your arms. I could turn you into an 'after.'"

I hadn't even realized I was lacking definition in the first place. "Am I a 'before'?" I agonized.

These days I am trying to accept and embrace "beforehood" and my imperfect status. Luckily and thankfully, I live a healthy lifestyle for the most part, and I am trying not to obsess too much over small flaws like a little belly or less-than-perfect arms. Life is too short to always be aspiring

soothe now

So what if everyone else is Spinning or doing advanced Zumba? If an exercise trend isn't right for you, take a pass. Your exercise routine shouldn't add to your anxiety but rather should be designed to reduce it.

toward bodily perfection, and a life with no wine, chocolate, or pasta (which are just a few things that the trainer was going to make me give up) is not worth being a perfect "after."

compete with yourself

Another one of my forays into the wide world of exercise was when I visited Tony Horton, the creator of P90X and a *very* tough trainer, for a workout.

Off the bat, he started, "How many push-ups can you do?" I said, "I can probably do about 15 of the hard ones."

Tony looked at me like I had insulted him. "Most guys your age can do 50 of them—at least 25." Wow, we were not starting off on the right foot! What did he mean by "guys your age"? How old did he think I was? What does age have to do with it? Why *couldn't* I do 25 push-ups?

At first I was insulted, but then I realized that Tony was probably trying to motivate me. It was then that I realized sometimes competition is arbitrary—strive to be your best, not to match others' bests. Over the next 90 minutes, Tony expanded on that point when he divulged his philosophy of getting into shape, which basically revolves around doing something that pushes you in a real way every single day. "It doesn't have to be crazy. If you can do 15 push-ups today, strive to do 17 or 20 tomorrow," he said. "Get a little bit of sweat going even if you only have 10 minutes. It all adds up." It's about competing with yourself, not others—otherwise, you're just causing yourself more stress!

how i soothe myself with exercise on the road

I'm famous for being on a diet and then beating myself up when I mess up, and it can get worse when I'm on the road for months at a time touring. I try to remember that there is nothing productive about kicking yourself. I'm only human. The next meal or workout is a new opportunity to get back on track. When I'm traveling, I try to stick to my regular program, knowing I won't find perfection.

When I can, I will go to the gym for a real workout as a way to deal with anxiety. Exercise is a prescription for so many stress-related issues. But on my last tour, I was exhausted all the time and made a deal with myself that a little extra sleep was more important than finding a gym on the road. However, I also committed to moving half an hour a day, even if it was just a stroll to a store. Or when I was at the venue, I'd walk up and down the stairs several times. I didn't blow it off, but I did give myself the leeway not to do a formal workout. On a visit with my parents, I wanted to spend real time with them and not leave for two hours to go to the gym. So I took a walk with them and we had time to talk. I was still moving, but I didn't lose out on quality time with them.

I also decided there would be absolutely no pizza on the tour bus. If you're not working out, try banning a favorite food that's high in calories—this helps you feel more in control of your body and less guilty when you can't squeeze in some movement.

If I have no time or very little space on the tour bus, I'll go outside and skip rope or just jump up and down like we did when we were kids. I'm not just moving my body, but also shaking off stress. If I can, I'll get the whole touring gang together for a day of biking or a group run. It's always easier to motivate yourself if the entire group is going along.

When I'm having trouble motivating myself, I read all I can about the benefits of exercise. Exercise releases endorphins, the chemicals we naturally make that produce what some call a "runner's high." Endorphins diminish the perception of pain and act as sedatives. When endorphins interact with receptors in your brain, a state of calm and feelings of well-being are produced. I remember this fact and know I'll feel better after I get a workout in.

soothe now

I recently tried yoga because every single soothing expert says that life is not complete without a few downward-facing dogs. Of course I have friends who do yoga all the time, so they push me to do it as well. Before I tried yoga, I had a fear of exercising with a group of people, but I knew I had to conquer it. So I went on Google looking for a yoga class in Cleveland and read about a 90-minute hot yoga class, which seemed incredibly frightening. A 90-minute hot yoga class? "Never, never, never ever. That's just not me," I said.

Sure, I could have given in to peer pressure and the trend toward hot yoga, but that's not exactly a great way to relax. That brought up an interesting topic for me: Can't I exercise on my own terms and not do what other people tell me to do? I'm through with yoga guilt!

soothe expert:

Larry Tedor on Soothing Through Movement

Here's what my awesome personal trainer Larry Tedor, AMP Fitness, Metabolic Coach, NPTI, NSCA, CPT, CNC, has to say about exercise.

MOVE AND SOOTHE

When tension rises, people can feel stressed or experience mild levels of anger. I prefer exercises that are more of a physical relief of stress. High-energy forms of cardio exercise such as boxing, resistance training, or group classes can provide an effective release of these negative emotions, turning these otherwise potentially unhealthy emotions into motivation for increased health and well-being. It comes down to the intensity level and the duration you stay at that level while working out. Exercise can decrease stress hormones like cortisol and increase endorphins, your body's feel-good chemicals, giving your mood a natural boost.

MEET YOUR FEEL-GOOD MOLECULES

The nervous system makes endorphins to diminish the perception of pain, making them to act like your body's own natural pain relievers. The receptors that endorphins bind to are the same ones that some pain medicines bind to. The result is that endorphins trigger a positive feeling in the body. The feeling that follows a run or a workout is often described as a "runner's high" because it's so euphoric.

RELEASE STRESS

Some exercises that I do with Jim at the gym or training studio can help relieve tension. I always ask Jim to do medicine ball slams, using a no-bounce medicine ball, or alternating rope slams using battle ropes. Both of these can be physical ways to get out aggression and release stress when you are on overload.

While you are at home, anything that gets you moving, raises your heart rate, and is done at a high enough intensity to release those endorphins is good. Make use of the things you have available, even if that means just your own body weight. Activities as simple as a combo of body weight squats with two quick boxing jabs (using dumbbells or cans of soup), jumping jacks, or biking work wonders.

EMBRACE CARDIO

Everyone complains about cardio, but I tell Jim that I prefer a workout that's cardio driven and performed at a higher intensity to keep your heart rate up, such as kickboxing, Spinning, or group resistance training classes. If you are able to up the rate to shed the weight, you will maximize your potential in reaching your fitness goals that much sooner. Adding some form of resistance weight to your cardio is crucial to raising your body's metabolism and losing weight.

I think for some people getting out and being in nature can be a stress reliever in of itself. It doesn't matter if it's biking, running, or walking the dog. As a mental stress reliever, such activities can be very relaxing, but if you are stressed both mentally and physically, you may want to consider something higher in intensity to release those endorphins.

AMP UP YOUR WALKS

In terms of weight loss, walking alone will most likely not get the job done, but it can be a starting point if you have been doing nothing as far as exercise goes. If you want to use it as a way to get in more cardio or to up your heart rate, you can try doing a fartlek walk, where you walk at a moderate pace and add bursts of speed walking for 30 seconds. Or try wearing a backpack filled with added weight to make your walk more challenging. However, a successful weight-loss program needs to include *all* parts of the puzzle: cardio, resistance training, and nutrition. One part is dependent upon the other. Most people need to exercise at an intensity level high enough to challenge themselves and keep their heart rate up.

GET MOTIVATED

In general, a good source of motivation starts with *setting small short-term attainable goals* that you can commit to. Surrounding yourself with like-minded people is ideal because you share the same values and can inspire each other through your own stories. Make your family and friends aware of your fitness goals; they can be huge sources of motiva-tion. If they know what you are looking to do, they will be asking about your progress and will genuinely want to see you succeed. Some other key things that can be great sources of motivation are workout partners and fitness professionals. Fitness professionals can hold you accountable for your actions, give you words of encouragement, teach you proper form, and be there to share their knowledge. Knowing that workout part-ners are counting on you for their own success can really help push you through a tiring day because nobody wants to let others down.

Taking before photos of yourself and posting them in places where you will see them such as on the fridge or the bathroom mirror also works for some people. A physical reminder of where you started it helps you keep moving forward. That's one thing I tease Jim about—having those pictures so he can compare and see his accomplishments.

FIND YOUR RIGHT TIME TO MOVE

Studies have shown that women benefit more from morning workouts to start their day out and balance estrogen levels, while men can reap higher benefits from afternoon or early evening workouts because of the boost of testosterone. However, it ultimately comes down to what fits into a person's schedule and with his or her lifestyle. You need to find that balance in life and make it work for you.

WORK OUT ON THE ROAD

Traveling can sometimes throw a wrench in the works, but if you plan ahead, you can get some activity on the road. Pack resistance bands or other items that can easily be put into your bag. You can also do a little research ahead of time to see if a gym or fitness facility is available to hotel guests. Even if you're short on time while traveling, you can get in a full workout with those bands and body weight exercises. I'm the guy in the airport lifting my luggage up and down as I walk to the flight, to simulate weight training at the gym.

STRETCH!

Stretching is a perfect form of exercise to incorporate into any workout program. Not only does it help keep your body limber; it can do double duty as a good mental stress reliever. Sometimes you are simply mentally drained, and the stress leaves you feeling overwhelmed and fatigued.

10

soothe your little (and big) freak-outs

The other day I was on a plane with this group of really loud fellow travelers who I believe thought they were filming the pilot for their own reality series. *"Hey!"* one shouted. *"Come over here!"* The other one shouted back, *"Don't bust my chops, Marie!"* All I could think was, *Wow. There are 200 other people on this plane. You're not home alone by yourself yelling across a backyard. You're in public.*

The more I thought about it (and the more yelling I heard down the aisles), the more I found myself getting stressed to the point where my blood was boiling and a headache was setting in. It took forever before a flight attendant went over to say, "A few people have complained. Can you please stop yelling?"

We've all been in public situations that seem to start out fine and then something happens that creates a stress cloud over the entire day. Have you ever been on a plane where the person next to you is reading a broadsheet newspaper and must spread out the pages over your lap, too? Or there's that guy at the gym ignoring the 45-minute limit on the treadmill. What about a restaurant that is dark, quiet, and lovely until someone asks to turn up the music?

Modern life is filled with so many stress-inducing moments that you could find yourself walking around stressed out all the time! I've learned that you must self-soothe, which means to take a moment and breathe. Remind yourself that you're not alone in the world and you will have to deal with people who might not live by your standard.

I did have to laugh when a friend of mine told me that last summer she was on train and someone nearby produced a toenail clipper and clipped his toenails all the way home to New Jersey, with the bits flying everywhere. When angry patrons gave him the evil stare, he continued his strange grooming ritual and just happily ignored them.

She said you could feel the tension, which made me remind her, "Did you take a moment, breathe, and try to get over it?" Sure, toenail man was pushing her buttons, but there was a way to take back the controls and return to a soothed state of mind.

Take a deep breath, calm your mind, and find peace in a chaotic world. For more on soothing your freak-outs, visit SootheYourWorld.com.

are you just being too judgmental?

When it comes to dealing with the public situations, I sometimes ask myself, *Is it just me?* Am I being too judgmental and allowing myself to get stressed out when I should just roll with it? I've almost come to terms with the idea that while I'm giving a concert, a cell phone somewhere will go off just when a song is reaching a beautiful haunting ending. *Breathe, Jim, breathe,* I tell myself. I think of Dr. Drew's meditative breathing exercise (see "Soothe Now: With Mindful Breathing" on page 10) and calm myself.

Honestly, maybe it is just me, which explains why I don't really want to go to the mall to look for a present for someone but instead jump on Amazon to avoid the crowds. Perhaps I'm the only one who avoids going to movie theaters on Friday and Saturday nights because I don't really want to smell those nachos next to me. I know it's far more soothing to go on a Tuesday evening, when the place is half empty. Maybe I'm just psyching myself up for stress that isn't necessary when I go to the airport and wonder what will go wrong today. Is it right for me to be stressed when I see some fancy car parked over three spaces when there isn't room in the lot for everyone to get one space?

I now try to recognize when I am judging according to my own standards of behavior, which might not be everyone else's laws of living. How can I learn not to put my values on other people's behavior? Do I say something to those who aren't doing what I feel is the right thing? Or do I just live with it and work on my own stress levels?

In regard to the situation on the plane, if I had said something to those loudmouthed talkers, like "Would you mind keeping it down?" . . . well, then what? I'm sure they would have directed their very loud opinions in my direction. My action would have resulted in a lose-lose situation.

life's little annoyances versus true injustices

I've decided that you must separate life's little annoyances from bigger, more important injustices—and most of what happens falls into the life's little annoyances category. For instance, I bought my parents a cruise, and at the last minute my dad couldn't go because he wasn't feeling well. Luckily I had bought trip insurance and expected to get my money back. Alas, after filling out the endless cruise-line reimbursement forms, I was informed that my claim was denied because I didn't read the small print about preexisting conditions, and since my dad had a preexisting condition, I couldn't get a refund. Honestly, this felt more like an injustice than a life's little annoyance, but I still had to decide if I was going to get stressed out enough to feel sick over it. In the end, I had to deal with it by not dwelling on it.

Would it make me feel better to call the cruise line and yell at someone on the phone who was just working at his or her job and not really in charge of the rules of its insurance policy? The truth is, yelling at the customer service rep on the other end of the call-in line might feel good for two seconds, but you're just pumping up your own blood pressure and upping your cortisol levels.

When I'm met with a "crisis," I lead myself through this exercise:

Inhale.

This isn't a life-changing event, but a pain.

This is just temporary.

You're not going to die.

Remember that life is a series of annoyances.

All I can do is control what I can control.

I'm never going to change anyone else's behavior.

And I will focus on the positive.

And I will do that right now.

Exhale. Slowly.

do you need forced relaxation to deal with your freak-out moments?

It's safe to say that I don't do vacations well. The idea of a week away is nice in theory, but I worry that I'll miss too much while I'm away. *I know, I know, I know.* You're supposed to use vacation as a way to unplug, undo, unwind, and all those other wonderful *un* things, but I'm unimpressed with the whole idea of forced relaxation. In other words, after I've been on vacation for about 15 minutes, you might have to tape me to that lawn chair because I'm the guy up walking around the pool and looking for a cell phone signal.

Maybe you're someone who counts down the days until you can put on a bathing suit and feel sand between your toes. I find that for me the only way to truly enjoy getting away is to travel far away, like to France. It's easier for me knowing that because I'm in a foreign country my cell phone doesn't really work that well and I'm truly not that accessible. That's when I can just walk around and see the sights because there is nothing else I can do.

I think you have to define your own vacation style. For example, I might freak out during a 10-day trip; I just know I'm missing too much good, exciting stuff at home. I've determined that when I'm really stressed, I need only three days away, the perfect weekend trip, to kick back. I can even put down the cell phone.

How else can you soothe your freak-out moments?

Remember that you're in control of your happiness. Studies show that we control a large portion of our happiness. While the environment accounts for 60 percent of our happy moments, we are in control of the other 40 percent. Use your control to sway yourself in the direction of not freaking out over the little things.

Make light of them. Listen to Scott Weems, the author of *HA! The Science of When We Laugh and Why,* who says: "What is important is humor, and for many reasons it reduces stress. It keeps us healthy. It even makes us smarter, so why not laugh?" Next time you're having a freak-out, take a moment to pause and try to find the humor in the situation, or the silver lining, to put it in perspective. If that is difficult, try watching your favorite funny video to enjoy a laugh and take your mind away from the freak-out.

Take an adult time out. Try what Nataly Kogan, cofounder and CEO of the wellness company Happier, advises. She says to pick a time in the middle of the day and set the alarm on your phone. When the alarm rings, step away from your work (desk, computer, phone) and take a few minutes to breathe, take a walk, or just have a chill moment doing what relaxes you, from a two-minute meditation to sipping some tea to just going outside to enjoy a nice breeze. This is not a waste of time, because studies show that when you're frazzled, you're 25 percent less efficient.

Live in the moment and pay attention. Matthew Killingsworth, a happiness researcher, says that being in the present moment will up your feelings of joy. Meanwhile, being mindful, paying attention to what's happening in the moment, will help you remain happier. It's a good way not to indulge in negative thoughts, but to glance at them and then dismiss them.

Always remember: This too shall pass. Remember that everyone has setbacks, but quite often people will have their biggest joys and breakthroughs after these down moments. If you can just get through this current struggle, figure that you will be that much closer to the happiness that lurks beyond it.

are you living in
"time famine" mode?

"I'm just too busy to allow even one screw-up."

How often do you think these words? Your entire day is hyper-scheduled and then the one glitch causes you to have a freak-out moment because one glitch in time will cause the whole day to fall like a row of dominoes. Maybe it's not the glitch that's the problem, but the fact that you have scheduled every single minute in your life. You honestly don't think there are enough hours in the day, although you make plans for almost all of that time. When a meeting runs over or your schedule is upset, then it's time to have a mini-meltdown, just as kids do when they don't get what they want. Maybe you take it out on your significant others or your kids or the people in your inner circle. They might even joke about the mini-meltdowns of yours that they have to endure, as in, "Oh no, Mom is about to have one of her meltdowns because Aunt Carol is late."

Experts are saying that we live in "time famine" mode most of the time, when we quickly bounce from one activity to the next without even building in a five-minute break. Some of us revel in this mode, gloating to others about how super busy we are, but hey, we feel good because we can do it all. I know one working mom who can never resist telling everyone that she's so super busy that she can't do this or that for fun. She can't understand why her friends rarely ask her to do leisure things with them anymore. It's not that she has pretty much shunned all those relaxing activities, but that they're tired of listening to her glorify her overloaded routine to them. Guess what? Everyone is busy, and trying to be the busiest bee of all is just stressful. Are you in a "busy competition" with your friends and family? Are you trying to outdo the next person when it comes to your schedule? The truth is, the only one who is hurting is you. "Excess business does cause stress, but people almost get addicted to the rush of having too much to do," says therapist Peggy Wagner.

If you want to shrug off some stress, stop reveling in your busy lifestyle and your long to-do lists. Instead try to look at the big picture of your day and plan for both productive times and relaxation moments. Giving yourself that downtime will allow you to be more productive when you truly are busy.

how do you know if you're too busy?

Here are a few ways to know you're too busy.

- You constantly brag about being so busy.
- You feel naturally competitive about being the busiest one of all.
- You see yourself as superior to your friends who are less busy.
- You find yourself repeatedly telling others how busy you are to the point where they're sick of hearing it.
- You feel super antsy if you do have a free day.
- You gloat on Facebook about every single busy moment of your day.
- Your friends "joke" that they don't even ask you to do something fun because you're "the busiest person alive."

soothe expert:

David "Yeah Dave" Romanelli on Dealing with Stress

Wellness innovator David "Yeah Dave" Romanelli is the author of *Happy Is the New Healthy* and *Yeah Dave's Guide to Livin' the Moment.* I asked him to share some of his tips for dealing with daily stress.

STOP MULTITASKING

Burnout is a huge issue in our culture. I think it's really important for people to focus on doing one thing at a time. The whole idea of multitasking doesn't really work. Scientific research into multitasking shows that not only does it make you less effective on the main thing that you're doing, but it also makes you less effective overall. It's not about being busy, but about showing up fully for whatever you're doing.

We try to stick to our schedules, but we don't realize that schedules are actually imperfect and often don't work out. The goal is not to be on schedule, but to be more present. For example, if your focus is to be with your kids, then really be with your kids and don't do eight other things at the same time. If you're at a meeting with your clients, then don't be on e-mail the whole time. If you are spending downtime, then really spend downtime and don't allow 50 interruptions. Show up fully and you will be more balanced and productive.

BUILD FOCUS

I just gave a talk for some executives at a major company. Afterward, they were outside smoking cigars, and one of them said to me, "Listen, I want to be that calm, focused guy you're describing, but it's really hard to be that guy. How do you do that?" One of the first steps is learning how to meditate. Meditation reveals the power of attention. People work out at a gym and develop their biceps. People who meditate build up their muscle of attention.

Our attention is basically tangled up in our thoughts. Have you ever had that experience where you're thinking about something that is making you unhappy or worried or anxious? One negative thought can quickly lead to another, and before long, you are in a downward spiral. You have the power to untangle your attention from those thoughts, right your mind, and put your attention into something positive. When you realize you have that ability to control your attention, it's an absolute game changer and the reason people swear by meditation.

OVERCOME NEGATIVITY

We notice the negativity around us when the negativity within us is the dominant emotional state. So the trick to overcoming negativity is an inner shift. There's a saying that it takes a real badass to be grateful. It's easy to wake up in the morning and focus on all the negativity in your life. The house is a mess. You're running late. Your back aches. It takes some serious mental strength to focus on the sunny day, the scent of your morning coffee, and the great music you are about to play to lift the mood. When you are an overwhelming force of positivity, you will force a change.

REWIRE YOUR BRAIN

There's a saying: "Neurons that fire together wire together." If you worry a lot, you become a world champion worrier who scans his or her mind to figure out something to worry about even if you're on the beach in the tropics. To escape that place of worry, it takes a concentrated effort to focus on the positive and change the neurocircuitry. To all the worriers out there, meditation is the best practice to initiate change and tilt your mind in a new and more positive direction.

CHOOSE LOVE

There are 1,440 minutes in a day. It's a powerful practice to dedicate one minute each day to love. I did an exercise where I walked around New York City with a film crew to see if I could get a one-minute hug from random New Yorkers. It was awkward at times, but one thing was clear. Everyone needs more love. Whether it's an uplifting e-mail or a pat on the back or a one-minute hug, love is the single most powerful way to spread positivity, disrupt unhealthy patterns, and show up fully.

11

soothe your looks (when you're super stressed-out)

I took a recent summer vacation for a week (I know, long for me!) with my parents and my brother. One day I was sitting on the front porch of this lovely rental house, and my dad said, "James, you're looking a little wrinkled."

Yes, that did get my attention, because I thought he was going to say that I finally looked relaxed. "It's a big problem when my skin looks better than your skin," Dad continued. "I'm 78, you know."

Then he said words I never figured would come out of my father's mouth. "Do you use Kiehl's?" he asked me.

When your 78-year-old father knows the elite brands of skin care, you really do have to wonder if the world has been taken over by alien forces. "Really, Dad, you know Kiehl's?" I quizzed him. "They have a great moisturizer. Prevents lines and wrinkles. With your stressful life, you should try it," he replied, and passed the grapes.

There's a great joke I heard about aging: It's good your eyesight starts going as you get older. That way you can't see the lines and wrinkles as much!

As if gravity wasn't enough, I've read all the reports about how stress manifests itself in physical ways, including making all of us look older, thicker around the middle, more wrinkled, or with bags and dark circles around our eyes.

As a performer in a world gone crazy with HDTV, I'm keenly aware of seeing my face on a jumbo screen. I also see my reflection often when I'm on tour, in the huge, wall-covered mirrors hotels love to use in their lobbies and rooms. Take it from me—don't bother looking at yourself in a hotel mirror after a grueling day of travel or a hectic business trip. You'll think you've time-traveled ten (or twenty) years into the future.

We all have to cope with daily stresses, but we don't have to wear it on our faces. I figured we could all use some help, so I went to some skin and body pros and asked for their quick stress-related fixes.

drink up

I'm not talking about wine here. There is a reason why all
these beauty experts talk about water, water, and more water.
By the way, neither soda nor those sugary sports drinks
count as water. You need pure water to help combat life's
daily stresses on both the inside and the outside. Joanna Vargas, skin-care expert to the stars, says, "Drink half your body
weight in ounces of spring water every single day." Let's do
the math. Say you weigh 150 pounds, which translates into
75 ounces of water, or nine cups a day. "Your skin really suffers if you're dehydrating yourself because you're not flush-
ing toxins," says Vargas. "You're probably walking around
dehydrated right now and don't even know it."

There is a simple way to figure out right away if you are
dehydrated. Just pinch the skin on the back of your hand and
hold the fold for three seconds, but don't do it super hard so
as to hurt yourself. When you let the skin go, see if the peak
from the pinch remains for more than a second. If it does,
then you are most likely dehydrated.

soothe now

There is good news if your jeans didn't fit this morning. If your body
is dehydrated, you'll actually trap toxins, which in turns means that
you truly are retaining water. This isn't an urban myth, but a fact.
Drink more and flush more . . . and literally flush more. That's how it
goes, or flows.

your good looks and stress

What does high-level (or even low-voltage) stress do to your beautiful skin and body? I don't want to cause any additional angst, but you should know that stress means the following to your physique:

You break out—at any age. Stress causes your adrenal glands to go into overdrive and start secreting the hormone cortisone. New York City dermatologist Neal Schultz, MD, explains, "Every time cortisone comes out, a little testosterone comes out as well. In women, any testosterone in the body is significant. Too much male hormone produces oil in glands, and that leads to increased acne."

The Fix: Exfoliate to remove dead skin cells and unclog pores. Another good way to avoid zits is to drink hot water with lemon juice when you know you'll be stressed out. It helps to do an internal detox, and skin care truly does begin on the inside. If you're prone to body acne due to stress, invest in a body brush. Do a dry (before shower) brushing of your body, which not only feels good and improves your circulation, but removes dead skin cells that blog pores and contribute to acne. Gently brushing your body is an incredibly calming exercise.

You lose your hair. It's true that heredity plays a big part in hair loss, but stress is right up there as a reason that you're seeing so many locks in the shower drain. Mental and physical stress produce too much testosterone in both men and women and cause stress-induced hair loss.

The Fix: Go to your dermatologist and ask about medication to manage the effects of too much male hormone. Sometimes he or she will prescribe a birth control pill because this balances the testosterone with more estrogen. Only your doctor can find the right balance for you. Other fixes that might or might not work are special hair-restoring

soothe expert:

Joanna Vargas on Skin Care

Joanna Vargas is a New York–based skin-care expert extraordinaire to the stars. I asked her how to look your best while traveling.

PREPARE FOR TRAVEL

I like to prepare well in advance for any vacation or business trip. This is because I can get stressed if I leave everything for the last minute. As we all know, stress makes a mess of your skin. So try to pack well in advance.

STAY HYDRATED

Once I get past security, I buy myself a water. If I'm running late, I order one the moment I sit down. You can also have soda water or green tea. Avoid V8; it's loaded with sodium and will not help if you want to stay hydrated. Push the button and ask for seconds if you feel you need it. I do anything to stay hydrated.

BYO PRODUCTS

Please do not to wash with that slimy bar soap on the sink! Your skin-care routine is vital, so don't forget to pack the basics—a face wash, an exfoliator, and a moisturizer.

DON'T FORGET SPF

Sunscreen is a must. This is especially true if you're going to a beach or a sunny location.

EAT FOR HEALTHY SKIN

Lean proteins and vegetables work. This gives your body the building blocks to repair itself and the nourishment for great-looking skin. If they have a juice bar, order a green juice to load up on antioxidants.

shampoos or supplements such as biotin or prenatal vitamins (which help hair and nails look good).

Your neck really hurts. Stress hits certain points in our bodies, and the neck is really prone to taking the brunt of a bad day. Not only are you stressed, but also the muscles in your neck are now so stiff that it hurts to keep your head upright.

The Fix: First, you should try to calm down with meditation because tensing up is what caused the muscle pain or spasms in your neck. Getting a professional massage can help, but if that's not available or is too expensive, try Kneipp hydrotherapy: Fill a tub with cold bath water and sit in it, then warm the water up, alternating between hot and cold three to four times. The idea is to loosen stiff muscles. Another way to do this is to go into a cold shower or splash cold water on the affected muscles for about a minute and then substitute warm (not hot) water. You're opening your blood vessels while also shooting blood to this area and removing lactic acid.

You get thick around the middle. Again, all that stressing makes your body store fat, plus when you're stressed, you're much more likely to reach for foods like chips and ice cream. All that comfort food isn't so comforting when your jeans suddenly don't fit.

The Fix: Since we all know that comfort food stored in our pantry "calls out to us," fitness expert JJ Virgin, CNS, CHFS, and author of *The Virgin Diet*, insists that you should do a complete overhaul of your fridge and cabinets and remove those types of foods. "You will eat them when stressed. If you keep healthy fruits and vegetables, you can reach for them and do far less damage," she says. She also suggests that you keep a small amount of dark chocolate on hand for true emergencies, but not go crazy eating it in the middle of the night just because it's there.

so many experts, so little time

You could read beauty and diet tips until the end of time, which is why I've culled a few of my favorites that really work for me and help me get through times where I'm super frenzied. This is what I do to try to look my best:

I do drink water. I know all the research about drinking half your body weight in ounces of water, but I think drinking even a little bit more water enables me to digest my food more easily and helps me avoid fake hunger pains. Most of the time, when you think you're hungry, you're actually thirsty.

I go green. Get me a green shake and I'm happy because I do feel like I'm doing something good for my body from the inside out. But I also make sure to eat a lot of greens instead of going for potatoes and rice as sides. I know the greens are good for my health, plus they make my skin look nice. So give me some raw or steamed kale and broccoli. I will admit that I actually do think these foods are tasty, plus all those phyto-nutrients can't be beat. Just combine some veggies into your omelet and you have a fast meal.

I don't do processed foods. I don't like to eat what I can't pronounce, and I know it's not good for my health, so I just skip it. This means that I actually read labels and always go for fresh if I can.

Yes, I do have an actual skin-care routine. I wash twice a day with a cleanser instead of bar soap. Afterward I'll always slap some kind of moisturizer on my face, which helps because I live in a cold climate and play concerts in so many

soothe now

Maybe you haven't gained weight, but your stomach seems to really pooch out when you're super stressed. Bloating is a way your body copes with stress: Because you are under stress, your body feels it might be in fight mode soon, so it is diverting blood from normal digestion and sending it to other muscle groups. What happens then is you feel bloated or perhaps have diarrhea. One good fix is to use an old-fashioned hot water bottle on your tummy to soothe those muscles. You also want to eat foods that naturally reduce bloating, such as almonds or a bit of parsley.

wintery spots on my holiday tour. I do wear a bit of powder onstage, and all the women who work with me have fits if I don't wash it right off. Believe me, I appreciate them so much because they know about good skin care. I'm not specific about products I use, despite my dad's insistence on Kiehl's. Just washing and moisturizing makes me, as a guy, feel like I've done enough in this department.

I do wear sunscreen. Of course as a kid growing up in Cleveland, I wore sunscreen only when I was at a pool for 10 hours. Now I know that it's important to slap on sunscreen to save your skin and prevent cancer. I'd love to say that I put it on every day, but I'm lazy. I am working on it, and I have heard that if you keep sunscreen in your gym bag and car (places where it's an easy reach), you'll be more likely to use it. I never go to tanning beds because of the obvious health hazards, plus I don't think they would allow me to bring my cell phone into one.

I do listen to crazy skin tips and think I might try them . . . someday. I have a ton of beauty experts on my weekend radio show, and they're always telling me the latest beauty tips. I guess if you're really stressed out and bags develop under your eyes, you don't have to walk around looking like a zombie from *The Walking Dead.* To reduce puffiness, just keep two metal spoons in your freezer and put the back of the spoon on each eye. I actually tried this tip and it worked (plus the cold felt really good). Another tip that sounds messier is brewing green tea and then allowing the tea bags to cool after you squeeze most of the water out of them. You put the cool bags on your bags. The ladies like this tip, but it sounds pretty messy to me, so I'll stick to the spoons.

I don't spend a ton on products. I just can't bring myself to spend $50 on a moisturizer when I can get something in the grocery store for $10. To that end, here's a tip on a cheap way to work on lines and wrinkles. Beauty experts told me to just buy some vitamin E oil in the grocery store or at GNC. Put a dab on any lines, wrinkles, or scars. This is what they use in most hospitals on scars to make them go away, and it really does work on your facial lines. I love that you can try it for under $5.

12

soothe with a little gratitude

In our busy world, I actually did something amazing a few days ago, which was to take a mini-vacation right in the middle of my day. I didn't have far to go because there's this path near my house in Cleveland that's a great place to hike. A few years ago, the city took the old train tracks and made miles of walking and biking paths as a way to help our community unwind and get healthy. On cool mornings or chilly fall nights after dinner, I love to go there because it's like a little forest in the heart of the city.

The other day was one of those humidity-free sparkling summer days when the rain has pushed the mugginess away, and all that is left was a refreshing breeze and miles of green grass, wise old trees, and a cloudless blue sky. "Instead of grabbing lunch, let's just grab a walk," I told a frazzled friend. And as we strolled on those well-worn paths, I could see that she was preoccupied, so I started pointing out the sights, big and small, as if I were her tour guide, although both of us have lived in the city most of our lives. At one point I stopped and said, "I'm really a lucky guy. This is a beautiful place, and I'm grateful to be in it."

I have to admit that I've been on hundreds of walks on that path, just taking all that lush nature for granted. Stuck in my own headspace, thinking about my week or my day or some future album, I would just walk along, my mind in overdrive. When we're stressed-out, we see very little and aren't grateful for much.

It's not exactly a joyful or aware way to live. It also raises the question: Are you grateful on a daily basis for all the wonder that is around you? It was humbling the other day when I heard someone say, "I'm so grateful that I'm out here walking around. There are people in the hospital right now, and others struggling with serious issues. I have absolutely no reason to be anything but grateful for my life."

Bells were going off in my mind; I had to agree.

If I could say one thing about myself now, it is that I'm grateful for all of it.

an attitude of gratitude

Actually, when you do something kind for others, you're the one who gets the positive mood-booster shot. A study by the Georgia Psychological Association showed that those who kept daily gratitude journals felt better about their lives than those who recorded hassles or neutral life events. Even those who kept gratitude journals on a weekly basis felt better, exercised more regularly, reported fewer physical symptoms, and felt better about their lives as a whole. They were even more optimistic about the upcoming week.

Someone suggested something so easy to me that I have to share it right here. What if you were to write someone a thank-you note today? This doesn't have to be a fancy card, but just a simple note or an e-mail saying, "I want to say thank you for . . ." Imagine how much this would brighten someone else's day, but here's the secret: It will also brighten your own.

I do know for certain that when you give more than you get, then everyone wins. Why not write: "I was thinking about you today and want to say that I appreciate you in my life." What if you sent out ten of those e-mails next week and start a gratitude chain event that touches your life and even the lives of those you'll never know? It's a small action that costs you nothing, but the gain here is beyond measure.

how about you start with a quick hello?

My friend Luke McMaster and I wrote a song called "Say Hello." I woke up in the middle of the night thinking of that song title for a simple reason: No one says hello to each other anymore. People feel like they don't have to say hello because we're already so connected online, right? We go from place to

soothe expert:

Dr. Drew Ramsey on the Topic of Gratitude

FIND TIME FOR GRATITUDE

When you focus on gratitude, you simply can't focus on your own stress. Plus, it's really easy to be grateful and do something nice for someone else. The practice of gratitude and giving is timeless. And it doesn't have to be complicated. Just hold the door for someone else. Say something nice to someone in your life or to a stranger.

CONNECT WITH GRATITUDE

What if you said to someone at work, "That's a really nice blouse you have on"? You would undoubtedly brighten that person's day. Thus begins a conversation and a connection based in gratitude. Having a connection with other human beings naturally soothes people. When I see people who are very agitated or unsoothed, in many cases they haven't had a conversation with another human being in a while. Make sure to connect with people through gratitude. It's the ultimate way of bonding.

place with our heads buried in our phones, avoiding human contact even when we're around other people.

Even when we're on a plane or a train, we don't look up from our electronics to say hello. And quite often we're so busy and stressed out in our lives that we'll call a family member or friend and get right to the point: "Hey, it's me. Meet you at seven. Bye." "I'll be there in ten minutes." You don't even need to call to get to the point because you can always send a quick text that avoids human connection even further.

The other day while I was walking around New York City, I noticed that no one even looks up anymore because their eyes are focused on their phones or they're taking photos of their lives at every minute instead of observing what's around them and living their lives. We walk around like little robots connected to our machines. Why would you even look up to see a friend and say hello? You certainly don't bother to say hello to a stranger because, chances are, there is no time for those interactions. Heck, there is no time for the people you *know*.

Luke loved the idea of this song because he first met his wife in a restaurant when he said hello to her. He engaged with her, and that was their beginning.

As for me, I know I'll never be one of those bright and cheery "good morning" people, but I am striving to say a simple hello to people because I'm grateful that I'm around them and want to connect with them. This doesn't mean I'm going to tell you my entire life story, but if we're put in a position where we share a close space, such as on a plane or in an elevator, I will say hello and acknowledge that you are there.

I've also made some great friends this way, including my friend Tom, a hand surgeon I met on a half-hour flight from Detroit to Cleveland. At first we did the typical guy nod, but eventually we said hello and introduced ourselves. Now we're friends and have something in common, since he works at the Cleveland Clinic, which is of course in my hometown. If he and I hadn't said hello and talked, I wouldn't have this interesting person in my life. Later on, when I was having some tingling in my hands and neck, he helped me considerably and then sent his assistant on the road with me to help because he's such a nice guy.

A simple "hello." That's all it took.

Are we so self-absorbed now that we can't greet one another or say "Thank you" or "You're welcome" because it takes too much time and effort? So what if the other person doesn't respond to your kindness? It still feels good within to say hello, smile, and then wait for the response. In fact, the other day I actually wondered if I was turning into my happy-go-lucky dad (but without those expensive Kiehl's products).

My dad says hello, refusing to take any of it too seriously, and smiles, walking away grateful for the day and the experience. That in itself makes me so grateful that he is my father.

This brings me to the other day on a flight, when I said hello to the flight attendant. She stared at me without a response and kept speaking with the other flight attendant about what they would do when they arrived in Los Angeles. I didn't walk away feeling rejected, but just laughed to myself because I knew something she didn't know: the power of a quick hello. I wrote a popular song called "The Gift," but the true gift is trying to make these little connections. I'm grateful for them.

one small thing

Here's a great way to show yourself some gratitude: Indulge yourself. In our busy lives, we usually don't stop for a moment to really indulge ourselves, and by this, I don't mean by buying a pint of ice cream and digging in. What is one small thing that you could do for yourself today? What is something you always wanted to do but never have done until today?

It doesn't have to be a huge thing, just one small thing that would make you grateful as you took a small chance at something new.

I always wanted to learn a foreign language, but talked myself out of lessons because they would be too time-consuming. Would I really learn to speak French in six weeks? Probably not. As is true with most people, I had that small thing that I wanted to accomplish, but I was just as good at talking myself out of it before I even tried it. Yes, speaking fluent French would be a huge commitment. What about learning a little French? Would that make me happy?

Along the same lines, I've heard that people take cooking classes at places like Williams-Sonoma, and I love to eat at home. I didn't really have the time for or want to commit to a six-week cooking class, but I vowed to do one small thing for myself and try a new recipe each night for a week. The rule was, it had to be something I had never cooked before, including a friend's pretty simple chicken and broccoli dish. I'd never baked a chicken and I didn't really know what to do with lemon peel, but I followed the recipe and the dish was absolutely delicious. I didn't decide to dump my day job to become a chef, but doing that one small thing for myself filled me with a nice feeling of accomplishment. I know this sounds silly, but I had no idea that I could just cut the chicken into cubes, throw the cubes onto a baking sheet with some broccoli, salt, pepper, and olive oil, and broil. Broil vegetables? Who knew?

Another one of my dreams is to become a good dancer. If *Dancing with the Stars* calls me today, I will admit to them that I have two left feet. In fact, I don't really know how to dance at all, even though as a kid I took mandatory ballroom dancing and etiquette classes. The dance lessons didn't stick. So forget going up in front of 20 million people on *DWTS*. However, I might consider taking a dance class in Cleveland as my "one small thing."

With these small things, I've decided that I don't have to be great at them, but hope to find stress relief and pleasure from just trying them out. What is the one small thing that you could do today for yourself? By the way, I do know enough French now to get through a vacation, plus I can roast veggies instead of just nuking them in the microwave. I'm not a gardener, but a few plants are surviving their life sentence in my backyard, and I know a few dance moves that might get me through a wedding.

I'm grateful that I've learned I don't have to be the best at everything. I can still enjoy the process of learning a few small things.

are you stressing yourself out over being the best instead of living in gratitude?

I love the show *CBS Sunday Morning*. The other day I was watching a segment in which an ordinary man professed that he was going to be the next Tiger Woods. He had never played golf before in his life, but he had decided at midlife that he would commit to being the best golfer in the world. Would he succeed? I wasn't so sure because being the best, I believe, is a combination of talent and teachings. So many factors contribute to making somebody a star of some kind. I wondered: Why couldn't this guy on the TV show say, "I've wanted to play golf my entire life. And now I'm taking lessons and playing a lot because I want to get out there and explore this sport while enjoying it."

You don't have to be Mikhail Baryshnikov to love to dance or mimic Carrie Underwood's high notes in order to be a good singer and enjoy music. Yet there is a mentality in our reality TV–crazed world that all you have to do is stand in line at *American Idol* and you are destined for superstardom. Wouldn't it be less stressful to decide that you're going to learn the most about something, enjoy it, and then see where it takes you? You just need to be involved in it—even without idol status.

When I was a little boy learning the piano, I had a teacher who told my mother that I had absolutely no aptitude for the piano and should stop taking lessons. "I don't care if he's

(continued on page 164)

soothe expert:

David "Yeah Dave" Romanelli on Gratitude

Dave knows the power of gratitude. Here are his tips for finding more in your life.

SHIFT YOUR THINKING

Philosophically, living with gratitude changes your approach from "What can I take?" to "What can I give?" The old adage is that wise men count their blessings while fools count their troubles. It feels so much better to focus on what's good in your life instead of what's not so good. Everything shifts when you live in gratitude. And it starts in an instant. If you're not grateful for what you have right now, how will you be grateful for what you hope to have in the future?

COUNT YOUR BLESSINGS ALL DAY AND NIGHT

Don't go to bed worried and anxious at night. Count your blessings. Take a few minutes as you lie down to think of five things for which you are grateful. This soothes the mind, puts everything into perspective, and truly helps you to fall asleep. And don't limit this to just a bedtime ritual. Throughout the day, stop and take a moment to say thank you for all that's good in your life. Here is the mantra: *Thank you. Thank you. Thank you.* Repeat.

GIVE YOURSELF A BREAK

I use 1:11 p.m. as a sacred time, and it's also a special time in numerology. I even set an alarm at 1:11. At that time, I push back from whatever is it I'm doing and enjoy. I'll enjoy the sunshine, savor a piece of chocolate, or listen to a Bob Marley song. In American culture, we put so much emphasis on work and productivity. That's not all bad, but it's not all good. We can take a cue from the ancient Eastern cultures, which are not as productive or modern, but more evolved and wise. They take more time to rest, to pray, to savor. Keep it simple. Take a little vacation . . . every day!

SPRINKLE GRATITUDE THROUGHOUT YOUR DAY

There is a study by Ed Diener, a professor of psychology at the University of Illinois, that shows that happiness comes from the frequency of positive experiences, not the intensity of positive experiences. In other words, true happiness and stress relief come from carving out little moments of peace and pleasure throughout your day. These moments don't take a lot of time or money. They take the discipline to push back from your desk and focus on the little things. I have a mantra: *A beautiful, funny, and delicious moment each day keeps the stress away.*

talented at all," Mom retorted. "It makes him happy, so keep teaching him. Let's see where this happiness takes him."

Along the same lines, are you stressing while planning to have the perfect dinner party with the right people and the non-clichéd food and the most interesting drinks? All that perfection is taking the joy out of what you're doing. Maybe you even avoid having that party because you know it won't be perfect. I don't cook in any way that would interest the Food Network, but I'll still have people over and ask someone else to make his fantastic guacamole while I take my best shot at the main course. We stress out when we make life a competition. When you do something for the joy of it, the pressure goes away and you can be grateful for the experience of it.

afterword

While writing this book about my search to find ways to soothe in life, my dad Richard passed away during my 2014 holiday tour.

I'm a real combination of my mom and dad. I get my tenacity, goal-setting and "anything is possible" spirit from my mom (oh, and my tendency to worry). My dad was an extremely happy-go-lucky guy, always laughing with a kind-hearted, welcoming smile. The charismatic life of the party. Although he worked very hard and had his fair share of ups and downs, he greatly appreciated the balance in his life, and truly loved the simple things. Richard Brickman's joy was in gathering together with friends and family, trying a new recipe, or going to the beach with his dog. I envied his ability to be in the moment, and just go with the feeling.

Growing up I remember him saying, "James, you need to have more fun. Don't take things so seriously. Enjoy life." But when I tried things that he or other people did for fun, I didn't think they were fun at all. My passion was playing the piano. It's all I ever wanted to do, and so in turn, I thought he didn't understand me. When I'd come home from a long concert tour he'd say, "You work so hard. Now you need to enjoy the fruits of your labor. Where are you going to go on vacation?" Then he'd list ten exotic places that he'd read about in the *New York Times* (reading it cover-to-cover was his daily ritual). I know that reading and learning helped him soothe. He wanted to make sure I enjoyed my whole life, or at least be open to the idea.

I believe my dad's greatest wish for me was to know that feeling of balance.

Over the past few years, I had the chance to spend some wonderful quality time with my parents. They traveled with me to Southeast Asia for a series of concerts, and came on cruises and to fan club events where my dad charmed everyone (he was the real star of the show). We even took a vacation to a farmhouse in France last year, something my dad always dreamed of doing, where we bonded through cooking, exploring, laughing and sharing stories in a way that makes me forever grateful for that time together.

Somehow when I least expected it, I discovered that my dad's soothing personality is a huge part of me. When I'm on stage, I feel his warmth and sense of humor come through me. His ability to gather people and sincerely make them feel welcome are gifts that I will carry throughout my life. Now I recognize that the best version of life balance is to find the passion and fun that suits each of us. This comes from the memories we create, the new things we try, the people and places that influence us, and the positive legacies we carry on from our parents.

In our last conversation, I joked with my dad about how I always knew when he was sitting in the front row of my concerts, because I could hear him laughing louder and longer than everyone else. He loved that! I'll miss so many incredible things about him: That big laugh, his wisdom and his presence. His affectionate and demonstrative ways, and his love and pride that will remain forever in my heart and in my music.

Until next time,
Jim

acknowledgments

I would like to express my deepest appreciation to all those who were a part of my quest to find soothe. I would like to thank Dr. Drew Ramsey, Amelia Love Hatcher, Tisha Morris, Kristin McGee, Peggy Wagner, Larry Tedor, David "Yeah Dave" Romanelli, Joanna Vargas, and Cindy Pearlman.

A special thanks to Homer and Linda Hickam and Patricia Cornwell for their thoughtful reads and kind words. Thanks also to Ellen Wohl, Claire Vanidestine, and the entire Brickman Music staff.

To my agent, Marc Gerald, and the entire team at Rodale, thank you for making this book possible.

I would also like to thank my family—my mom, Sally, my dad, Richard, and my brother, Michael—for their unending love and support.

This is just the beginning of my soothing journey.

discography

No Words, March, 1994, Windham Hill Records.

By Heart: Piano Solos, April, 1995, Windham Hill Records.
Certified gold by the Recording Industry Association of America

Picture This, January, 1997, Windham Hill Records.
Certified gold by the Recording Industry Association of America
Features the hit song *"Valentine"* with Martina McBride

The Gift, April, 1997, Windham Hill Records.
Certified gold by the Recording Industry Association of America.
Features the hit song *"The Gift"* with Collin Raye and Susan Ashton.

Destiny, January, 1999, Windham Hill Records.
Certified gold by the Recording Industry Association of America
Features the hit song *"Love of My Life"* with Michael W Smith

My Romance: An Evening with Jim Brickman,
August, 2000, Windham Hill Records.

Simple Things, September, 2001, Windham Hill
Records.

Valentine, February, 2002, Windham Hill Records.

Love Songs and Lullabies, August, 2002, Windham
Hill Records.
> Features the hit song *"You"* with Jane Krakowski

Peace, September, 2003, Windham Hill Records.
> Grammy nominated for Best Instrumental Album.
> Features the #1 hit single *"Sending You A Little*
> *Christmas"* with Kristy Starling

Greatest Hits, May, 2004, Windham Hill Records.

Grace, April 19, 2005, Windham Hill Records.
> Features the hit song *"Hear Me"* with Michael Bolton.

The Disney Songbook, October, 2005, Walt Disney.
> Features the hit song *"Beautiful"* with Wayne Brady.

Escape, October, 2006, SLG Records.
> Features the hit song *"Never Alone"* with Lady
> Antebellum.

Christmas Romance, December, 2006,
Compass Productions.

Homecoming, September, 2007, SLG Records.
> Features the hit song *"Coming Home for Christmas"*
> Richie McDonald of Lonestar.

Hope, 2007, Somerset Entertainment.

Unspoken, September, 2008, Savoy Jazz.

Faith, 2008, Somerset Entertainment.
Grammy nominated for Best New Age Album.

Ultimate Love Songs: The Very Best of Jim Brickman, January, 2009, Time/Life Music.

Beautiful World, September, 2009, Somerset Entertainment.

Joy, October, 2009, Somerset Entertainment.

Home, November, 2010, Somerset Entertainment.

Love, 2010, Somerset Entertainment.

All is Calm: Peaceful Christmas Hymns, 2011, Somerset Entertainment.

Romanza, 2011, Somerset Entertainment.

Believe, November, 2012, Somerset Entertainment.
Features the hit song *"Good Morning Beautiful"*

Love 2, January, 2013, Somerset Entertainment.

The Magic of Christmas, November, 2013, Somerset Entertainment.
Features the hit song *"Sending You A Little Christmas"* with Johnny Mathis

Timeless, August, 2014, Somerset Entertainment.

On A Winter's Night: The Songs and Spirit of Christmas, October, 2014, Green Hill Productions.
Features the hit song *"That Silent Night"* with Kenny Rogers and *"Night Before Christmas"* with John Oates

collaborations

Kenny Rogers, Martina McBride, Gerald Levert, Lady Antebellum, Michael W. Smith, Kenny Loggins, Carly Simon, Herb Alpert, Collin Raye, Michael Bolton, Sara Evans, Donny Osmond, Olivia Newton-John and Johnny Mathis.

PBS specials

My Romance: An Evening with Jim Brickman, 2000.

Love Songs and Lullabies, 2002.

Jim Brickman at the Magic Kingdom—The Disney Songbook, 2005.

Beautiful World, 2009.

Celebration of the 70's, 2013.

Index

Underscore references indicate boxed text.

about the author

JIM BRICKMAN is recognized as the best selling solo pianist of our time, selling over seven million albums worldwide. Since his debut release *No Words* in 1994, Brickman has received two Grammy® nods, two SESAC "Songwriter of the Year" awards, the coveted GMA Dove award, and four certified gold albums by the Recording Industry Association of America—*By Heart, Picture This, The Gift* and *Destiny*. Brickman hosts *Your Weekend with Jim Brickman*, a weekly radio show, and is a strong supporter of PBS, starring in five concert TV specials for the network.

Brickman is the author of two motivational books, *Simple Things* and *Love Notes*.

JimBrickman.com
SootheYourWorld.com
🐦 @JimBrickman
📘 JimBrickman
📷 TheRealJimBrickman

CINDY PEARLMAN is the author of the new YA fantasy trilogy, *Ascenders* and co-author of the best seller *Jex Malone*. A well-known entertainment journalist, syndicated worldwide through the *New York Times Syndicate,* she also interviews A-listers for the *Chicago Sun-Times*. Cindy has authored and co-authored over 40 books including *Simple Things* and *Love Notes* with Jim Brickman. A movie-loving kid in Chicago, she grew up to earn a degree from the Walter Cronkite School of Journalism at Arizona State. Cindy lives in Nevada and can be reached at Bigpixnews@aol.com.